Jihadist State

&

Social Cohesion

Anthony John Cowley

ISBN: 9781549875267

Dedication

"To the men and women of the security, military and police services whom stand guard at the gate, who steadfastly defend and protect our freedoms from a world of chaos and self-righteous violence, tyranny and fascism, the common enemy of humanity. They protect our rights of expression, free association, justice, honour, in a free society for all the people".

AJ Cowley

"Tolerating evil leads only to more-evil and when good people stand by and do nothing while wickedness reigns, their communities will be consumed."

Bob Riley

Preface

Terrorism of all kinds has been practised throughout the ages, it is only due to recent events which have taken place over the last fifty years that this fact has come to light. Scholars of history and humanities have been aware of this but for the rest of us Long John Silver in Treasure Island and currently the adventures of Jack Sparrow in Pirates of the Caribbean have entertained us for a number of years, the truth of the matter is, it has been very much the opposite in real life and memories of the past are lost as generations go by.

It is with interest, therefore, to know that during the period of the sixteenth to the nineteenth century, Europe and the United States were terrorised by the Barbary Pirates (Privateers - Corsairs). Prior to 1776, all American and British flagged merchant shipping was protected from the Barbary Pirates by the Royal Navy, after American independence from Britain this cover was sporadic and during the 1790's a tribute was paid for the safe passage of vessels by the US.

Barbary pirates of North Africa were sponsored by the Arab rulers of Morocco, Algiers, Tunis and Tripoli. In this endeavour, they had been tasked to capture ships and demand a ransom, take seamen as slaves.[1] This led to two wars between the

[1]These acts did not surface again until the rise of Somali Pirates in 2009

United States Navy from 1801–1805 and again in 1815, the main targets were the Ottoman Corsairs and the Mohammetan Pirates, the first middle east military intervention by the US.

Jihad, a no-compromise offensive war in seventh-century Islam, wars against Spain and Portugal 711–1492 on the Iberian Peninsula. The Muslim invasion of France in 732, which was repulsed, Sicily and large parts of Italy. Muslim armies repeatedly invaded Europe but were finally driven out for the last time in 1683.

The supremacy of one religion over others, the Qur'an, an allegedly holy book full of superstitious horror, with primitive textual verses, a divine tool of authoritative justification, coupled with fascism resulting of what is two faces of Islam. The rights of Muslims to subjugate non-believers, with a religious duty to spread Islam through "dawah" – "the call", meaning persuasion and reasoning, some admit it means conflict, in self-defence and against oppression, an Islamic tactic for waging Jihad: "taqiyya" or "kithman", lying, deception, deceit, encouraging Muslims to lie for the good of Islam.

Wahhabi a mentally unstable sect run by Quranic fundamentalists, uncompromising in their belief in ruthless pursuit against disbelievers, but merciful to one another. What Muslims must do is use verses from the Qur'an to justify hatred, violence, rape, murder and genocide. Children are "schooled", this is a loose interpretation you understand, from a very early age in this seventh-century ideology, how else are they to feed the death cults of al-Shabaab, Kataib Hizbollah, Hamas, al-Qa'eda, Boko Haran, Isil, Haqqani Network. Strangely in the eleventh century from Syria and Iran came Hash-Shashin, an Islamic sect that murdered very important people and gave the term "assassin".

How will current terrorist acts shape our society and individual freedoms in the coming years, it is important from a sociological viewpoint that not all Muslims are tarred with what is a very wide brush, as the majority follow "Monotheism," who prefer treaty and form relationships with those that do not follow the Islamic faith. It is important that the Non-Muslim section of our communities give support to them, there are a few in our society who would like to drive us apart and create the mayhem that would follow, they are keen to see what Enoch Powel described and noted as the "rivers of blood" speech, actually come to fruition on our streets.

On the sixteenth of January 1979, the Shah of Iran fled into exile, in the November of the same year up to 600 militants planned to overthrow the Saudi government, the militants walked into the holiest place in Islam, the Grand Mosque of Mecca and sized it. Having taken one-hundred thousand hostages the stand-off lasted two weeks, this hostage situation influenced the formation of Osama bin Laden's, al-Qa'eda which changed Islam forever.

The attackers were all Sunni Muslims from Egypt, Jordon, Somalia, Canada and the United States of America. Their leader Juhayman al-Utaybi who declared himself the prophesized leader the "Mahdi", whose sole role was to cleanse the Muslim world.

The US blamed Ayatollah Ruhollah Khomeini, the leader of the Iranian revolution for the seizure, in turn Khomeini accused the US and Israel, and many people in the Muslim world began violent protests, the US embassy in Pakistan was burned to the ground. The siege at the Grand Mosque ended when Saudi troops, the National Guard along with French special forces stormed the mosque with tanks, heavy artillery and poisonous chemicals, the outcome of this produced thousands of casualties.

April the thirtieth 1980, six men seized control of the Iranian Embassy in London and took twenty-six people as hostages, which included embassy workers, BBC staff, tourists and a police guard. These men were members of the Democratic Revolutionary Front for the Liberation of Arabistan (DRFLA).

They demanded independence from Iran's Khuzestan province and the release of political prisoners held in Iran, after six days of slow negotiation and frustration they killed one of their hostages, and threw his body out of a window, the SAS were sent in to resolve the situation, during this operation five of the six terrorists were shot dead and one hostage killed in the crossfire.

Qur'an Verses:

English Translation – The Quranic Arab Corpus
http://corpus.quran.com/translation

2:65, 2:154, 2:193, 2:191, 2:216, 2:217, 3:28, 3:56, 3:85, 4:3, 4:24, 4:84, 4:89, 4:100, 4:101, 5:33, 5:51, 5:59, 5:60, 7:166, 8:12, 8:39, 8:60, 8:65, 8:67, 8.72, 8:73, 9:14, 9:5, 9:20, 9:29, 9:30, 9:33, 9:36, 9:39, 9:41, 9:73, 9:111, 9:123, 16:106, 17:16, 22:19, 24:13, 25:52, 29:69, 33:50, 33:57, 47:4, 48:29, 58:3, 60:4, 61:9, 65:4, 66:9, 70:30, 98:6

Sahih International

3:169 – 3:171, 47:5 – 47:15, 69:30 – 69:33

Disbelievers:

"Strike them over the neck and smite over their fingers and toes. Strike them on their foreheads to tear them apart and over their necks to cut them off and cut off their limbs, hands and feet".

Allah

Contents

Prologue

Islam a Brief History   1

Chapter 1

North Africa   7
  Morocco   8
  Algeria   12
  Tunisia   17
  Libya   20
  Egypt   23
  Somaliland   27
   Djibouti   29
   Somalia   31
  Ethiopia   34
  Eritrea   36
  Sudan   38

Chapter 2

Middle East   41
  Iraq   42
  Iran   47
  Turkey   56

Chapter 3

Asia Pacific   69
  Southeast Asia   70

Chapter 4

    The Dark Side of Islam   78

Chapter 5

    Your Inner Jihadi   89

Chapter 6

    Life in a Caliphate   99

Chapter 7

    Good Bye Jihadist World   112

Epilogue   123

Source Material

    Bibliography   129

Prologue

Islam a Brief History

The first recorded Muslim mosque in Britain, was in Liverpool in 1889, it was founded by Willian Henry Quilliam a solicitor. He converted to the Islamic faith and with a donation from Nasrullah Khan crown prince of Afghanistan, he had converted a number of terraced properties to become the first functioning mosque, which was called the Liverpool Muslim Institute. In the same year, the first purpose-built mosque was completed in Woking, Surrey.

Mohammed (570–632) born in Mecca in Saudi Arabia, he was left as an orphan and was brought up by a poor but kind uncle. He often went to Syria with trading caravans, as he grew older, he thought seriously about all that he saw and heard in the desert and in the cities as he travelled about.

The matter which caused him the deepest concern was the ignorance and superstition of the Meccans and other Arabs who had no ordered religious faith. He married a rich widow named Khadija and became a merchant. During Mohammed's time, there were both Jewish and Christian communities in Southern

Arabia. Mohammad grew familiar with the teachings and lives of Jesus Christ and the Jewish prophets. He saw visions and claimed that he was directed by God, through the archangel Gabriel.

At the beginning of his mission, Mohammed, like other prophets he was fiercely opposed by his own family and was subsequently persecuted by others that his life was in peril and he was forced to flee to the city of Medina two hundred and fifty miles to the north, where some of his supporters who had seen the writing on the wall, had already fled.

The date of his departure from Mecca is significant for the Muslim faith (July 16th 622). This date is used by the whole of Islam as the commencement of the Islamic calendar. It was also a turning point in Mohammed's career, he had proclaimed himself as the true interpreter of God and as a prophet he persistently preached his own doctrine.

At Medina the Jews were powerful and Mohammed thought that he could combine with them in furthering his new worship, but the Jews refused. After winning a powerful position in Medina, he declared war against both the Jews and the Meccans. When the Arabs began to flock to his standard, he sent messages to neighbouring Kings, some of them accepted Islam as the Mohamedan religion, which was to be properly called "Islam" which in Arabic means "submission to God and his divine will". Others refused and wars were declared against those who tried to check the teachings of Islam.

After the conquest of Mecca all Arabia embraced Islam, non-Muslims were not allowed to enter Arabia and he sent letters to all the Kings of Europe and Asia calling upon them to acknowledge that "there is no God but Allah and Mohammed is his prophet". Mohammed died in Medina in 632 just ten years after his departure from Mecca, his tomb in Medina and the city of Mecca are places of pilgrimage for all Muslims.

Within one hundred years after Mohammed's death, Syria, Persia, Egypt, North Africa and Spain had been conquered by Mohammed's successors called "Caliphs". Today Islam is the faith of and in excess of, one and a half billion people.

Islam's holy book, the Qur'an teaches the oneness of God, it lays down the boundary between God and human beings. It prohibits gambling, drinking alcohol, eating pig meat and applying high rates of interest on money lending. It teaches brotherhood and equality to all, whatever their creed or whatever their religion may be and kindness towards the weak, slaves and orphans. The Qur'an states clearly that women have the same rights as men, including the right to hold and inherit property. In various Muslim countries however, these rules are not strictly observed and practices differ widely.

The Qur'an teaches religious toleration and reverence to all past prophets, including Jesus and Moses and to holy books. Muslim's may not deny or dishonour any of them. Islam abolished priests, insisting upon direct communication between God and man without intervention. The Qur'an condemns monasticism and stresses cleanliness of body and soul.

Every Muslim is commanded to strive to develop his mental, moral and spiritual sides. Another duty is to pray five times a day facing towards Mecca. The muezzins or criers, give the call to prayer at dawn, at noon and sunset. One month a year called Ramadan is kept as a season of fasting where Muslim's may not eat between dawn and dusk. They are permitted to have as many as four wives at one time, provided that the strictest conditions laid down are duly observed.[2]

Islam has many sects, Sunnites or orthodox Muslim's and the Shiites, the Shiites insist that the descendants of Ali, husband of the prophet's daughter Fatima, are the only legitimate caliphs, or leaders of Islam. The Saracens, followers of Islam passed from Africa into Spain in 711, exactly one hundred years after Mohammed's death the Muslim invasion of France was halted by Charles Martel, driven back into Spain on the west and held in check by the Byzantine Empire at Constantinople, the Arabs, Moors and other Muslim peoples settled down in their new-won

---

[2] The loss of males in a population through famine or war, and abandonment.

lands and developed a culture which far surpassed that of Western Europe from the eighth to twelfth-centuries.

Among other centres of this culture was Damascus in Syria, Baghdad on the Tigris, Cairo on the lower Nile, Cordova in Spain and Delhi in India. The Saracens were excellent craftsmen, the sword blades of Toledo and Damascus were world-renowned. Equal skill was shown in the fashioning of vases, lamps, and other articles of copper, bronze and silver. The weaving of carpets which are still very highly sort after and world-renowned. Production of fine glass and pottery and a leading form of Muslim art was developed in architecture, the arabesque decoration of walls, carpets and hangings, took the place of drawing the human figure, which was severely restricted by tradition in Islam.

Sweetmeats, syrups, essences, perfumes were produced, along with paper without which printing would not be possible and the finest leather goods came from Cordova and Morocco. In literature and in particular poetry and in science the Muslims attained a high degree of development. In Spain, in the tenth-century a library of four-hundred-thousand manuscripts is said to have been collected.

Learned Arabs did much to preserve and spread the writing of Aristotle after he had been all but forgotten in Western Europe. In mathematics especially Algebra, Muslim scholars led the world. They were also responsible for Arabic numerals used today, which they brought from India to western Europe. In astronomy, medicine and chemistry they made notable advances.

Chapter 1
North Africa

Morocco

The Moors were originally the native inhabitants of Mauretania, an African province of the Roman Empire. The people were Berbers, an early Christian white race. Mauretania became Morocco, the Moors today are of mixed blood and are Muslim inhabitants of North West Africa.

Moors are better known to the British as corsairs or pirates of the Barbary coast, who in the sixteenth and seventh centuries preyed on merchant shipping, their attacks were so widely carried out they penetrated into English and Irish waters. Still earlier "Morris" dancing, which at one time a much wilder pastime than it is today, it had been introduced into England by travellers who had learned it from the Moors of Spain. Behind this lies a fascinating history, Arab armies sweeping across Northern Africa in the seventh century, encountered the Berbers, who they converted to Islam and joined forces to invade and subdue Spain.

The Moors enjoyed some medieval periods of brilliant civilization, where their achievements had a more direct influence on the western world. In Spain, the Moorish rulers were generally tolerant in their treatment of the native Spanish, although they always remained an alien aristocracy, they made no effort to convert the natives to Islam. In central Spain, the powers of the Moors were broken in 1212 by Alfonso VIII of Castile, at the battle of Las Navas de Tolosa. The Moors continued to hold Granada until 1492 when it was conquered by Ferdinand and Isabella. Most of the Moors were driven out, and the remaining were badly persecuted in spite of promises of fair treatment.

It was this persecution which roused the Moors out of Africa to "sea-revenge", this was due to the strength of their number not being sufficient enough to attempt a land re-conquest, this produced the "corsairs" to wage an unending war against Christian ships from Iceland to Egypt. The most famous of these pirates was Khair-ed-din Barbarossa, who was in fact, a brilliant seaman, comparable with the great English and Dutch admirals. The corsair movement quickly degenerated into a shameless piracy, which was not finally suppressed until the French conquest in North Africa in 1871.

The largest Moroccan towns are Casablanca, Marrakesh and Rabat, remains of their greatness are still to be found in Spain, the best of which is the Alhambra palace at Granada. During the opening years of the twentieth century, European nations and the United States, regarded Morocco simply as one of the threats to peace in the world.

As it transpires that analysis was correct, the Moroccan Islamic Combat Group and its affiliates, form the largest terrorists and insurgent groups in Afghanistan, Iraq and throughout Europe and the Middle East, driven by global Jihad and deteriorating social and economic factors.

A Daesh plot using chemical weapon attacks, in order to sow within the population "an attitude, by violent antisocial acts, where a person's perception of reality is severely distorted" the aim of this madness is to steer the population into revolt and dissolve the government in Morocco allowing them to install an Islamic caliphate.

The Taliban, former Mujahideen in Afghanistan run franchises rather like running an everyday business, one of many of these franchises in North Africa is a concoction of who's who in terrorist groups, al-Qa'eda in the Islamic Maghreb are led by mainly Algerians and are linked to al-Shabaab, with a splinter group known as al-Mourabitoun run a media outlet known as al-Andalus, where they peddle their doctrine.

The Moroccan Islamic Combat Group, a Salafi Jihadist group and their affiliates, are the wealthiest and the best-armed group. This they have achieved by kidnap, ransom, document forgery, arms trafficking and the illegal drug trade. The ransoms paid from western governments and humanitarian organisations run into tens of millions of dollars and the illegal trade in drugs spans the globe, they are active in Brazil and on the borders with Argentina, Paraguay and in North America, Canada.

They were involved in the Casablanca bombings where thirty-three people lost their lives in 2003, they struck again in the Madrid train bombing with one hundred and ninety-one people died and some two thousand injured. Let there be no doubt that with forged documents and illegal drugs they have positioned themselves, wherein, such places as the jungle in Calais, where they are able to spread throughout France and Spain. The removal of the jungle may turn out to be a double-edged sword, helping potential jihadists to spread their ideology and at the same time give them a much greater opportunity to blend into the population and this would likely result in a rise in terrorist atrocities.

Algeria

Named after its capital Algiers, the Algerian coastline is eight hundred and fifty miles long and forms part of the North African coast, it has a narrow strip along the Mediterranean Sea, this is a strip of highly fertile land. The population is over forty million, the indigenous inhabitants are Arabic Berbers. This intensively cultivated and densely populated strip, is called the "Tell", it follows the Mediterranean Sea for the whole of its length, the Tell produced in the 1920's, cotton, tobacco and olive oil for export, but for home consumption they cultivate wheat, barley, oats, maize, potatoes, beans, peas, tomatoes and in the warmer lowlands tangerines, bananas, pomegranates, almonds, figs and dates.

Apart from the Tell, the country south of the fertile coastal strip are the high plateau lands which have no agricultural value. This part of the country is populated by wandering tribes, sheep, goats and cattle which graze on coarse grass and aromatic herbs, these being the only form of vegetation.

South of the plateau region is the Atlas Mountains which cut diagonally across the country from Northeast to Southwest. These mountains are rich in minerals, iron, zinc, lead, copper, mercury and antimony. The country has the second highest oil reserve in Africa and is the ninth largest natural gas reserves and is a member of the OPEC oil-producing countries.

In the twelfth century Algeria was absorbed into the expanding world of Islam, in 1518 the Turks conquered the country which remained under Turkish rule for three hundred years. Later the port of Algiers became the headquarters of the Barbary pirates. These pirates made up the mob, who preyed on Mediterranean shipping with crews slaughtered or sold as slaves. Christians were kept a prisoner in the dungeons of Algiers, Tunis and Tripoli. In 1816 Lord Exmouth with a small British and Dutch fleet, destroyed the defences of Algiers and set the slaves free. Surprisingly this mob of cutthroats managed to terrorise the Mediterranean shipping for three hundred years complicit with its Turkish rulers.

In the lands of the Islamic Maghreb, there have been kidnappings by terrorist groups working along the border between Algeria and Tunisia, these groups started out as the Armed Islamic Group of Algeria. A splinter group was formed in 1998 called the Salafist Group for Preaching and Combat, they gave their support to al-Qa'eda in 2003, the founding members were veterans of Afghan Jihadis returning from Afghanistan.

This Islamic movement is involved in a gorilla campaign through the use of car bombings and assassination, the use of false roadblocks and ambushes have in the main occurred in the mountain areas, these practices are now happening along the border regions to the South and Southeast. South of Algeria became known as the "Triangle of Death" their ideas for killing civilians included unveiled women, which was orchestrated by their magazine al-Ansar from London.

The group tried to influence Algeria's general election with the threat of "one vote, one bullet", to be carried out by a breakaway faction, called the Islamic League for Da'wa and Jihad. In Britain, Algerians were arrested in a number of cities amounting to and in excess of ten since 2001, the cities of Leicester, Glasgow, Edinburgh, Manchester and London.

In London 2003 a cell was caught producing ricin and a police officer was killed in Manchester. Algerian jihadists returning from Afghanistan came to London, amongst them Abu Qatada who took over the weekly magazine, "Usrat al-Ansar" which became a trusted publication and information for Islamist terrorists around the world. Algerians were arrested in Spain, Italy, France and Germany all from the Salafist Group for Preaching and Combat. The growing concerns around the concentration of Algerians in London, with the ability to tap into the Moroccan Islamic Combat Groups expertise, in the production of false documents to fund logistical support specifically passports and visas, with credit card scams providing hard cash, the lax border controls in Britain made this all too easy, asylum and illegal immigrants from Calais and if it were not for the French applying pressure, the Finsbury Park Mosque would still be in the hands of the Jihadists. Abu Hamza and Abu Qatada activities included using false paperwork supplied to them in sending many to Afghan training camps, who subsequently have then returned to Europe.

The Algerian Islamic Front, this splinter group has an indoctrination process which includes those selected into the Islamist circle, are then sent to Afghan training camps only to return. In Canada one operative was stopped at the border with the United States, he was attempting to cross the border driving a car bomb, his destination was Los Angeles in 1999. Some of the members of this group were arrested in Leicester, they were given a prison sentence in 2003 for eleven years, the question is "where are they now"?

Salafists Group for Preaching and Combat, this group tends to stay clear from Algeria, this above all is to avoid all contact with the countries border authorities, due to the protracted asylum process which makes it possible to detect any false paperwork and with a high degree of certainty over a correct identification of them.

Other unscrupulous groups include the actions of Jund al Khilafa "Soldiers of the Caliphate" in Algeria by suggesting that beheading is perceived as a strong brand-building activity, that other groups might use this method to cement their position on the side of the Islamic State.

Tunisia

Tunisia in North Africa has a history going back some three thousand years, it is bounded on the north and east Mediterranean Sea, to the southeast is Libya and to the west is Algeria. The country is mountainous with deserts to the south, the valleys to the north are well cultivated and produce cereals, oranges, figs, grapes, almonds, dates and olives. Other than agriculture they engage in wool spinning, carpet making, sponge fishing and copper-ware. Minerals from phosphate rock are exported and other minerals include lead, zinc, iron and manganese.

Most of the people are ninety-eight per cent Muslim Arabs, there are a small population of Jews and Christians and one per cent Berbers, the total population is over ten-million. In its history, it was a possession of Egypt and Tunisia was later occupied by the Phoenicians who in the seventh century BC founded the city of Carthage near what is now the city of Tunis. The power of Carthage was broken in 146BC by the Romans who called the region Africa and made it the granary of the Roman Empire. Passing into Arab rule in the seventh century AD and in 1575 sized by the Turks till 1705, then in 1881 it was conquered by the French, it was recognised as an independent monarchy in 1956, a year later this was abolished and Tunisia became a republic, the Tunisian revolution in 2011 saw the over throw of its president Zine El Abidne Ben Ali. This was followed by parliamentary elections which was repeated in 2014.

Tunisia is a non-NATO ally of the United States and a member of the United Nations, with close relations with Europe in particular France and Italy. Tunisia's oil production is modest in comparison with its neighbours, but additional exploration has revealed potential new oil and gas fields.

The country is undergoing economic modernization offering investment incentives to foreign businesses, including a free trade zone with the E.U. The country's emphasis is on their most valuable income from the tourist industry, the older textile sector which saw a steep decline during the western economic disaster from 2007, has shifted to the higher quality goods market.

The Arab spring in 2011 saw the collapse of an authoritarian regime in Tunisia, the country had been under the cosh by the Islamist group Hizb Al Nahda party, a Salafist group who had been banned because of an overthrow attempt in 1992, they were granted legal status in 2011. In 2002 a bombing of a synagogue on the Tunisian island of Djerba, which has a large Jewish population, resulted in the deaths of two French, Five

Tunisians, and fourteen Germans. In 2009 two al-Qa'eda terrorists were put on trial in France for the 2002 bombing.

Other Islamic terrorist groups abound, with clashes in the border regions in 2006 and 2007, a number of clashes took place between the militants and security forces. The main terrorists are the Tunisian Combat Group, who are a radical offshoot of Al Nahda, who operate outside of Tunisia. This group has ties with al-Qa'eda in the Islamic Maghreb, who were formally known as the Algerian Salafist Group for Preaching and Combat, this group actively recruit Tunisians for Jihad abroad, and in 2009 Tunisian expats were arrested in Afghanistan, Pakistan, and Iraq. All of the suicide bombings in Iraq for a whole month was down to a network in Tunisia.

Since the start of 2015, there has been a surge of Islamist terrorist attacks, this has left Tunisia with serious challenges, the terrorist recognises the tourist industry value is central to Tunisia's interest and by interrupting that value gives credence to their cause and therefore get the bulk of public attention.

Libya

This huge empty country mostly desert has a population of six and a half million. The country is bound by Tunisia and Algeria on the west, on the south by Nigeria and Chad, on the east by Egypt and the Sudan.

In 1951 Libya became an independent federal kingdom, set up by Britain and France through the United Nations. The majority of the people are Muslim Arabs. Libya is a Greek name and is mentioned in the Odyssey by Homer, he describes it as fertile but having only seen the coastline, it is in fact a thin strip along the coast that is cultivable. The vast hinterland is one of the hottest and most barren regions in the world.

Libya has been inhabited by the Berbers since the late bronze age and was in-fact early Christian until the fall of the Roman Empire, in a seventh-century invasion brought the Arab colonisation and Islam. In the sixteenth-century the Spanish and the Knights of St John occupied Tripoli, until the Ottoman Turks arrived in 1555, which then became a nest of pirates as the Turks exercised no control over the population. Libya was involved with the Barbary wars in the eighteenth and nineteenth century's. Libya had been occupied by the Italians from 1911 through to 1943 until they and the Germans were defeated by the British eighth army in El Alamein. The country became an independent kingdom in 1951 until a coup in 1969 saw the overthrow of King Idris, when the country was taken over by Muammar Mohammed Abu Minyar Gaddafi, who ruled from 1973 until he was killed in the civil war in 2011.

During the Arab spring in 2011, the economy of Libya crashed due to the main source of income from oil stopped. Although Libya was a member of OPEC long-standing economic sanctions placed on them by the United Nations, prior to the Arab spring and the disruption to oil production by the continuous warring factions had a very negative effect and the country's health system, along with its financial centres failed. Libyan oil reserves are the largest in Africa along with natural gas and gypsum. It was estimated that in 2011, it would take ten years to rebuild the infrastructure. The international community is unwilling to provide humanitarian aid, this is due to the competing administration's inability to put together a coherent plan nor agree to a government of national unity. There will be no clear vision to address the populations aspirations as the economy suffers from chronic structural unemployment with a significant reliance on immigrant labour and a lack of economic diversity only produces popular unrest. In an effort to improve the economic outlook the United Nations lifted the sanctions on oil exports in 2011, this act jumps started the Libyan economy and by 2013 it had recovered to half of the previous high in oil output and by 2015 was nearly back to pre-2011 output levels.

MI6 have warned that the Libyan arms dumps have become a one-stop shop for world terrorists. Al-Jama'a al-Islamiyah al-Mugatifah bi-Libya or more commonly known as the Libyan Islamic Fighting Group who are affiliated with al-Qa'eda.

They fought the Soviets in Afghanistan, and are still operating today, their main goal is in using the current uncertainty to bring about a Caliphate in Libya. The country is still a hotbed for Islamic Jihadist groups, like al-Qa'eda in the Islamic Maghreb affiliate Jabhat al-Nusra and the soldiers of Ansar al-Sharia, including the Shura council of the youth of Islam. These Jihadist groups have used the current political chaos to regularly mount attacks on the Libyan security forces along with the Mujahideen in threatening Libya's parliamentarians, in 2014 they forced the parliament in Tripoli to relocate, without a central government the pressure on the local population is forcing them to acquiesce to the Jihadi groups.

Egypt

Egypt is somewhere near to three hundred and eighty-six thousand square miles, but only fifteen thousand square miles are inhabited. The Nile delta is a fertile strip set in a vast desert. Egypt has one of the longest histories of any modern country, with a population exceeding ninety-two million people.

The Egyptians are nearly all orthodox Sunni with a minority Shia Muslims, with the exception of the Copts who are Christian, they are descended from the ancient Egyptians but never converted to Islam. The Coptic church is one of the earliest forms of Christianity.

Egypt's economy is vast in comparison to other North African nations but has the largest population with five million immigrants, mostly Sudanese with a small number coming from Iraq, Ethiopia, Somalia, South Sudan and Eritrea. Stateless people, refugees and asylum seekers number two hundred and fifty thousand, registered Syrian refugees' number above one hundred thousand. This is especially significant when taking into account the average Egyptian earns around $2 per day in 2017.

The Suez Canal is one hundred and twenty miles long but is only wide enough for one-way traffic, it has two passing points, in 2015 an additional section of twenty-two miles had been completed, allowing for separated passing in both directions. Egypt produces oil and gas and is the largest non-OPEC producer in Africa and currently planning its first nuclear power station. Tourism is one of the most important sectors of the economy, with one of the seven wonders of the ancient world still in existence, with the beach resorts of Safaga, Sharm El Sheikh, Hurghada. Nile cruises from Luxor to Cairo with numerous cultural places along its length makes it a popular destination for tourism.

Egypt went bankrupt in 1876 and in response to this Britain and France took over the Egyptian finances, there was resentment over this and Europeans were massacred in Alexandria and in 1882 the British landed troops in Egypt in response to this act. British rule dated from the victory over the insurgent Arab Pasha at Tel el Kabir, at the same time Egypt was suffering from fanatical religious rebellion in the Sudan. The Egyptian army of ten thousand was wiped out in 1883, by the rebel leader Mahomed Ahmed, the "Mahdi". General Gordon was killed in 1885 in Khartoum, it was not until the Sudan was finally pacified and established under the Anglo-Egyptian Sudan was the Mardi dealt with.

Egypt was still nominally part of the Turkish empire, although the British had a standing army in the country. When the Turks joined the Germans in 1914 Britain annexed Egypt.

This did not last and in 1922 Egypt was made independent, in 1936 a treaty was signed for the defence of the Suez Canal zone until 1954 when the canal zone evacuation was agreed as Egypt became a republic in 1953.

This agreement was going well until 1956 when Egypt nationalized the international waterway and refused access to the Israelis. Israel struck first, the Egyptian army crumbled, the next day Britain and France gave an ultimatum to both parties, Egypt refused and the Suez crisis began with British and French airborne troops deployed to capture the canal, this was thwarted by President Nasser who ordered that a large number of ships to be sunk laden with cement, effectively blocking the canal to shipping, this was so effective, that the canal was not cleared until 1957. Diplomatic relations had been broken off, a number of foreign banks and businesses had been seized and nationalized by the Egyptian government.

The Egyptian economy has not fared well since the Arab spring in 2011, with a downturn in domestic oil and gas production, the economy was facing difficult times and political uncertainty having a direct effect on tourism and foreign investment. During the intervening period, Egypt's political transformation has forged ahead and the consequences of which the government has attracted fund management investment. The current trade deficit has narrowed, but the budget is under stress from subsidies and rising wage bills, the introduction of tax evasion measures is to be toughened. In 2017, Saudi Arabia is providing investment to help resolve the public deficit, but subsidies for food, electricity, and gas are steadily cut adding to cost inflation.

On the terrorist front, the country faces several groups such as Ansar Jerusalem "supporters of Jerusalem" who are based in the Sinai Peninsula. Ansar which is also known as Ansar Beit al-Maqdis, is the deadliest of the current crop in Egypt. Since the ousting of the Muslim Brotherhood, they have carried out car bombings in Cairo, also they are responsible for downing aircraft by using portable MANPAD anti-aircraft missiles, with attacks on tourist coaches and the disabling of gas pipelines. The government sees Ansar as the same face as the Muslim Brotherhood, Ansar has issued a fatwa declaring Egyptian soldiers as infidels.

Somaliland

Somaliland as it was once called, is a region which is referred to as the Horn of Africa, which has Rass Xaafuun as its most easterly point. The country is washed on the north by the Gulf of Aden, on the south-west by the Indian Ocean. Its land borders touch Ethiopia everywhere except in the south-west where it meets Kenya.

Most of the interior is a barren plateau, with peaks reaching some six thousand feet which descends into broken hills down to the coastal plains, which vary in width from thirty to sixty miles. The chief vegetation is a coarse grass, stunted thorn and acacia trees. In the 1960's the wealth of the Somalis, who had a nomadic lifestyle with large herds of camels, goats and sheep. The country was divided into French, British and Italian Somaliland, now called Somalia. French Somaliland, now called Djibouti, the most northerly, has an area of eight thousand one hundred square miles, and for the most part, hot and barren. The French Somaliland in 1954 had a population of one hundred and sixty-seven thousand, with thirteen thousand Europeans.

British Somaliland to the east of the French section, it was an area of sixty-eight thousand square miles, Britain first established a protectorate in 1885-87. A legislative council with elected members was set up in 1959 as the first step to self-government. The capital was Hargeysa with the chief port of Berbera. At that time, the population varied between thirty-five thousand and seventy thousand in the towns, while the nomadic inhabitants numbered sixty-eight thousand. The country's chief exports were meat, hides, gums and livestock.

Italian Somaliland was the largest part of the interior at one hundred and seventy-eight thousand square miles. Large areas are unproductive except where the rivers Webi Jubba and Webi Shabeelie provided narrow strips of land for cultivation.

From 1901 to 1920 trouble occurred in the British sector by the followers of a local Muslim leader who became known as the "Mullah". During WWII, Italian forces advancing from Ethiopia in 1940 forced the British out of the country as they were heavily outnumbered, but seven months later British troops landed in Berbera and drove out the Italians in Somaliland. In 1950 Somaliland was handed back to the Italians under a United Nations trusteeship for ten years, by 1957 it had been virtually self-governing and was to become independent in 1960.

Djibouti

Djibouti gained independence from France in 1977, after an independence vote a year later it joined what is now the African Union, later the Arab League and the United Nations in 1986. The current population is eight hundred and forty-six thousand, and predominately Sunni Muslim, the life expectancy is less than fifty years. The country's economy is concentrated in its deep-water ports in the service sector. The ports handle the bulk of domestic and foreign trade, it acts as an international refuelling and transhipment hub.

The economy has limited capacity for agriculture and industry, it is also suffering high unemployment not helped by one thousand illegal immigrants and high foreign debt. Djibouti has few natural resources, salt from Lake Assal which is exported, all the country's electricity is generated by fossil fuels, but has the potential to generate via geothermal energy. The overall trade deficit is high due to its limitations in agriculture and manufacturing as these goods are required to be imported. Exports include re-exporting of aircraft parts, homegrown animal hides and live animals. Important trading partners are France, Somalia, Ethiopia, Gulf States and China.

Al-Shabaab in Somalia, an insurgent group linked to al-Qa'eda, Djibouti is seen as a legitimate target because of its support to the Somali government and its participation in the African Union peacekeeping mission, also the country hosts the biggest base for the United States in Africa. Suicide bombers are targeting football matches, transport hubs including any crowded areas such as bars and restaurants.

Somalia

Ongoing civil and political unrest are preventing the government in developing coherent economic activity. A lack of authority in the rule of law, caused by different authorities and militias applying completely different sets of legal frameworks. Corruption and the lack of transparency have resulted in government revenues being embezzled. Somalia living standards are among the lowest in the world, with traditional livestock, agriculture and fishing being the only legal economic activity.

The core of the ongoing civil unrest are conflicts over land grabs by warlords and the inevitable displacement of local populations. The civilian judicial system has collapsed and non-functional. The government is unable to provide basic services, coupled with the inability to collect duties and taxes, which severely constrains productive economic activity. The result of all this is that Somalia is a stateless conflict-ridden economy.

Somali pirate's activities started in the 1980s when the civil war was at its height, and more importantly, the Somali Navy was disbanded leaving no at sea policing. Between the year 2000 and 2014, the pirates have plied their trade by attacking shipping and demanding ransoms. Today the country is in free fall and it's a case of every man for himself, the Puntland region the home of the pirates has been very busy indeed, but very much under the radar, so what has been going on?

What started the whole process of piracy was the indiscriminate dumping of toxic waste in the fishing grounds, this caused the fishermen to look for what they could do to eek a living, so they started to hijack the vessels operating in their fishing grounds, this quickly moved to much larger vessels as it became a lucrative money pot. This all changed when the United Nations set up the anti-piracy initiative, where a number of foreign governments decided to act and to protect shipping and take the pirates head on so to disrupt their trade.

Al Qa'eda linked al-Shabaab and the Somali ISIS faction was having a hard time as the cost of arms was very high. It's not all that clear when this started to change but change it did. Who spoke to who is unclear, there is a high possibility that al-Shabaab has asked the pirates to provide a delivery service for them, as weapon smuggling across the Gulf of Aden brought the price of arms down to less than fifty per cent of what they had been previously.

The warlords, as it turns out are not of the usual type but are just as vicious as the name suggests. They are in fact business men and government officials, who are providing licences to fish the waters off Somalia for vast fees. The licences are going to Iran, South Korean and Thailand, they have large fleets of fishing vessels and are not concerned about net sizes or conservation of fishing stocks. The Somali pirates have cottoned on to this and are offering to protect these vessels for huge protection fees, so the pirates are supplying terrorist as well as running an extortion racket from shipping. Strangely an oil tanker had been hijacked in Somali waters, the first time in five years in 2017, a call to the police from the Puntland region to the pirate crew, informing them that this vessel was working for a certain individual who was to be nameless. They were told to let the ship go or else, with the promise that they would not face any consequences for their actions. They complied.

Ethiopia

With Italy's support, Ethiopia was accepted as a member of the League of Nations in 1923, although France and Britain were against this because Ethiopia was still a feudal state and still had slaves. Ras Tafari was proclaimed "King of Kings" as Haile Selassie. His country was overrun by Italy in 1935 and went into exile until British forces drove the Italians out in 1941. On his return, he modernized the government and abolished slavery. Ethiopia joined the United Nations in 1952 and in order to improve foreign relations, Haile Selassie paid state visits to many countries, including Britain in 1954. On the occasion of his Silver Jubilee in 1955, he proclaimed a new constitution which gave the country its first general election in 1957.

The capital, Addis Ababa, at the very heart of the country and is eight thousand feet above sea level. In 1957, the city had a population of four-hundred-thousand inhabitants. It was connected by a railway that was finished in 1917 to all the chief towns and ports. The economy at that time revolved around, sheep, goats and herds of cattle as the wealth of the people, except in the valleys the country was too dry and arid making it unsuitable for agriculture. Ethiopia's main valuable export was coffee which was a product native to the region, grown in the forests of the south-west.

In 2015 the cash crops include coffee, pulses, oilseeds, cereals, potatoes, sugarcane and vegetables. The country has deposits of coal, opal, gemstones, kaolin, iron ore, soda ash and tantalum, only gold was mined in significant quantities.

The population is one-hundred and four million, with a life expectancy of sixty years. Ethiopia is a Marxist-Leninist regime that has practised government terrorism since the overthrow of Haile Selassie. Relations between Muslim and Christian have been quite cordial, indigenous Muslims have not been receptive to Islamic radicalization. It is true to say that Cristian and Muslims are geographically intermixed over most of the country. It is also true that the government has a tough and very effective security system, many of whom are veterans of previous and very recent conflicts. They have firm and harsh tactics and above all corruption is very low.

Ethiopia is not the soft touch unlike its neighbours in the Horn of Africa, the society in general, is one that has little or no access to the internet and mobile telephones, as these are rare and due to the lack of this technology, these shortfalls are not conducive to terrorist communication.

Eritrea

A strip of land six-hundred and fifty miles long and seventy miles wide to the west of the red sea, called by the Romans "Mare Erythraeum" also called Eritrea by the Italians. The coast is very hot but the mountains of the interior have a pleasant climate. The population in 1960 was a little over one million being half Cristian and half Muslim.

During WWII British forces occupied Eretria in 1941, where it came under a British military government. The United Nations took the decision to federate with Ethiopia in 1952, though it retained local self-government.

Eritrea has an extensive amount of mineral wealth, such as copper, gold, potash, granite and marble. The war of independence from Ethiopia between 1998 and 2000, the indiscriminate use of landmines has resulted in a decline in agricultural productivity. After the war manufacturing infrastructure was rebuilt and now includes, beverages, processed foods, tobacco, leather, textiles, metal products, chemicals, salt and paper products.

The current population in 2017 is over five and a half million, the country has an authoritarian government and a militarised state. The life expectancy is around sixty years old, with poor economic conditions which still continue to fuel illegal migration, predominately the young, it is thought that more than four thousand flee the country every month in search of a better life.

The country is a hotbed of state-sponsored terrorism, the government has been accused by the international community of bankrolling Somalia's pro al-Qa'eda terrorist group using British bank accounts. This money also funds al-Shabaab in carrying out atrocities in Ethiopia and Kenya. The government is proactive in proxy conflicts between Ethiopia and Somalian government forces, the Eritrean government conceives plans and supports and directs external terrorist operations.

It just does not stop there, they have their intelligence agencies operate in the Sudan and Uganda and should al-Shabaab manage to topple the government in Somalia, there would be a big risk that an Eritrea-Somali force re-visit a conflict on Ethiopia, this could result in the whole of the Horn of Africa in conflict with each other and a conflict backed by Iran.

Sudan

The Arabic name "Beled-es-Sudan" means "the country of the blacks". The people of the north and south are sharply differentiated, in the north are dark-skinned Arabic speaking Muslims who make up the majority of the population, the south is of negroid stock who have a tribal life and speak a central African language, but in 2011 the government of the south included English as an official language of the republic.

The Sudan from 1899-1955 was under a joint British-Egyptian rule, Britain approved self-rule for the Sudan and a draft constitution was drawn up in 1952, this was agreed by Egypt and a pact was signed in Cairo in 1953. The following year the first independent parliament was opened, two years later the machinery of government had been fully transferred and a republic was proclaimed in 1956.

The Sudan is the largest country in Africa at two and a half million square kilometres, its capital is Khartoum. It has land boundaries with the Central African Republic, Chad, the Democratic Republic of the Congo, Egypt, Eritrea, Ethiopia, Kenya, Libya and Uganda. The ethnic groups in the north are Arab-Muslim and Christianity in the south, the infant mortality rate is eighty-three per thousand, with a life expectancy of fifty-two years.

Sudan's natural resources include modest oil reserves, natural gas, gold, iron ore, copper and other industrial metals. Agricultural products include cotton, peanuts, sesame seeds, gum Arabic, sugar cane, millet and livestock. In the north which covers most of the Sudan, holds most of the urban centres. The southern region is predominately rural-subsistence economy in the south contains many more tribal groups.

A religious leader named Muhammad ibn Abdalla in 1889, proclaimed himself the "Mahdi" or the "expected one" and began a religious crusade, his followers are named Ansar's "the followers", which continues to this day as the single largest political grouping the Uma Party.

Sudan had a direct link with al-Qa'eda, Osama bin Laden was settled there between 1991-96, whereby he left for Afghanistan. A group called the Janjaweed have not been labelled as terrorists as they are supported by the government but are cited as engaging in terrorist acts against civilians.

In Darfur in 2003, while the north-south conflict was well on its way to a resolution, increasing reports of attacks on civilians, especially non-Arab tribes in the marginalized region of the Sudan. The government of Sudan increased arms support to local tribes and militias known as the Janjaweed, mostly Arab-

Muslims who killed three hundred thousand people in Darfur, including two million displaced people, the violence was nothing more than genocide, the mere talk of an impending attack resulted in a population displacement.

Chapter 2
Middle East

Iraq

Two great rivers, the Tigris and the Euphrates flow across the land between the Syrian desert and the Iranian plateau down to the Persian Gulf. At their lower courses, the two rivers have created a fertile plain which was known previously as Mesopotamia "the land between the rivers" a cradle of civilization where for centuries peoples and cities rose to power, here Sumerians and Babylonians, Macedonians and Persians once held sway. Baghdad, the caliphs once ruled the mighty empire of Islam only to be replaced by the Ottoman Turks.

During WWI, saw the ousting of the Turks from all Arab lands by the British and Indian armies, aided by Arab tribesmen,[3] who had risen in revolt. The League of Nations made it the nucleus of a new treaty with British administration under a mandate. In 1921 the Emir Feisal was proclaimed King of the new state of Iraq with its capital in Baghdad. In 1932, Britain's mandate was ended and relations between the two countries were governed by a treaty previously signed in 1930.

A new twenty-year treaty of alliance initiated in 1948 was rejected by the Iraqi government, later in 1955 Iraq joined with Turkey, Britain, Pakistan and Iran in signing the Baghdad Pact, a

---

[3] Aided by TE Lawrence

defensive alliance which was intended to promote peace, security and prosperity in the Middle East, after only four years Iraq formally withdrew in 1959.

During WWII, there was an attempt to form a pro-Nazi regime in Iraq, British troops restored order and Iraq subsequently declared war on Germany. In 1948 Iraq joined forces with other Arab League countries in a brief and unsuccessful war against the Jewish State of Israel.

Feisal II was sent to be educated at Harrow school, he returned to Iraq and became crowned King in 1953. In 1958 following the establishment by Egypt and Syria of a United Arab Republic, Feisal and his cousin King Hussein of Jordon united their two countries in a similar way as the Arab Federation, which Feisal was head, until it was dissolved by the Iraqi military who killed the young King, his family and advisors in 1958.

The country is one hundred and seventy-two thousand square miles, the population is over thirty-seven million, the official language is Arabic-Kurdish and the main religion is Islam. Iraqi oil economy in 2017 ranks second in the world to Saudi Arabia and is a founding member of OPEC.

The Iran and Iraq war between 1980-88 was a culmination of both internal and external factors, there had been a long history of border disputes and insurgency after the Iranian revolution, the desire of Iraq to replace Iran as the dominant Gulf State ended in Iraq invading Iran in 1980.

WWI tactics ensued using trench warfare and from 1982-88, Iran was on the offensive. Iraqi forces using human wave like attacks coupled to the extensive use of chemical agents, the Iranian forces on the front line were not the only target, their civilians were bombarded with chemical weapons. Twenty thousand Iranian soldiers were killed by nerve gas, later sarin and cyclosarin were used on the Kurdish city of Halabja.

The Gulf war in 1990-91, saw Iraq invades Kuwait in the summer of 1990, a one-hundred-hour operation Desert Storm land war ensued expelling Iraqi forces. Yet again WWI tactics brought into action with a fortified defensive line in the desert called the "Saddam Hussein Line" those defending suffered large losses as US armoured bulldozers buried the defenders in their trenches. Following this loss, Iraqi forces used Scud mobile missile launches to strike at Israel and Saudi Arabia.

At the cessation of hostilities, Palestinian workers and their families were forced to leave the country due to Yasser Arafat support for Saddam Hussein and Saudi Arabia expelled Yemeni workers for their support of Saddam.

The Gulf War of 2003, Operation Iraqi Freedom was as a direct result of failing to comply with United Nations resolutions, continuing government attacks on the Kurds in the north and the

Shi'a Muslims in the south, no-fly and no-drive zones were implemented in those areas to protect these populations. More importantly, the United Nations Security Council required Iraq to surrender, destroy and submit to inspections of its Weapons of Mass Destruction. Iraq's failure to comply left the US-led coalition no option but to invade.

At the start of the campaign and during, some parts of the US and coalition troops had chemical sensors register low-level counts, which was put down to storage facilities being bombed as the cause, and subsequently there has been a large number of medical studies into returning troops health.

After the conflict had ended Shiites returned from exile, shortly after, Shiite and Sunni sectarian violence erupted, caused by cleric Muqtada al-Sadr. Sunni tribesmen who had formerly fought against US troops realigned to counter insurgents affiliated with al-Qa'eda. Iran was providing direct extensive military aid to Shiite militias participating in Iraq sectarian conflict in 2010. In 2011 the US military withdrawal from Iraq, allowed old disputes between the Sunnis, Shiites and Kurds fight over territory, power and resources for overall control. Later the insurgency that started in 2003 had reincarnated themselves in the form of the Islamic State in 2011.

In the autumn of 2017, the Iraqi forces are defeating the last pockets of resistance by ISIS fighters, but the writing is already on the wall for another ISIS due to the scale of frustration, lack of hope and the lack of government. Who after all is going to oversee the rebuilding of the cities that have borne the brunt of the violence and destruction?

The same old story, it seems, ISIS militants reappearing in their neighbourhoods after being detained and then freed, corruption within the security and judiciary, as Islamic State Fighters have bought their freedom from jail.

Kurds are pressing ahead with independence against strenuous objections by Iran, Turkey and the US, starting a fresh war before the other has finished as tensions are raised between the Kurdish peshmerga forces and Iranian-backed Shiite militias over the borders of Kurdistan.

Iraqi Kurds have taken control over areas which was once controlled by the Iraqi government, in these areas, the Kurds will not acquiesce control where they feel that they have shed blood over. Indeed, nor will they accept the presence of Iranian backed Shite militias, as US-allied Kurdish peshmerga fighters have clashed with them in Tuz Khurmatu.

Iran

The country of Iran has a long history of change and chance in an ancient land and is over six hundred and thirty-six thousand square miles, with a population in excess of seventy-seven-million of mixed race mainly sixty-one per cent Persian, sixteen per cent Azeri and ten per cent Kurds with five smaller groups making up the remainder. The religious majority are mainly ninety per cent Shia and nine per cent Sunni, with some small sections of Jewish, Christian and Baha´i. Infant mortality is forty-three in every thousand with a life expectancy of 70 years.

Iran's physical features in the western half of the plateau are crossed by numerous mountain ranges, salt and sandy deserts cover about two-thirds of the plateau area. Salt Lake Urmia, which is threatening to dry up, The Caspian Sea in the north, with the Persian Gulf and the Gulf of Oman in the south. The economy is based on the country's oil wealth with minerals such as iron, copper, tin, lead and coal, with salt, rug and carpet manufacture. Agricultural products include wheat, barley, cotton, tobacco, rice, beet sugar, fruit and nuts, by products of silk, wool and hides, opium and gums.

With the ousting of the Shah in 1979, revolution resulted in the formation of the Islamic Republic of Iran, which was ratified in the same year. In 1980-88 the Iran-Iraq war transformed the political landscape. This war was costly to those who took part, especially on the Iranian side, as they had not seen trench warfare before on such a large scale. The Iranian army had conscripted young boys and prepared them for the front line, they aged between nine to sixteen who had volunteered to become Martyrs, they were employed to run over the front lines and collect landmines that had been laid by the Iraqi forces, they would then break through the Iraqi lines before they detonated the mines, this would be prior to an Iranian ground attack, this was all done while shouting "Shaheed" "Shaheed" (Martyr, Martyr).

Iran has two military forces which are required to maintain internal order and protect its borders, the Islamic Revolutionary Guard is tasked with this. The Qods Force is a clandestine branch which has the task to cultivate and support terrorist groups abroad, they provide weapons and training and above all funding to groups such as Hamas and other Palestinian terrorists, Lebanese Hizbollah, Afghanistan Taliban, and Iraqi militants.

During 1981, Iran was involved with the overthrow of the Bahrain government, in 1983 was involved in the bombing of western embassies in Kuwait, the worst excesses were to take place during the Islamic Holy Pilgrimage "hajj" in Mecca. Iranian so-called pilgrims rioted in the vast crowds, causing chaos, death and injury. Iran was at the centre of attention, as they provided training and assistance to the Saudi Hizbollah, in the 1996 attack on US military accommodation in Saudi Arabia, killing and wounding five hundred people including two hundred and forty-seven US military personnel. The scene was set for what was to follow, it cannot be ruled out that the Iranian government was involved in the setup and training of the Saudi based terrorists, that attacked the World Trade Centre in 2001, now known as nine-eleven. Possibly supporting financially with living costs and flying training in the US and at the same time providing false documentation.

The US government has also been complicit in funding a number of groups in Iran, possibly the Mujahideen-e-Khalq in 1997, in reprisal for the military loss in Saudi Arabia, the year before, but soon afterwards, placed the same group on their terrorist watch list. This action could be seen as the "CYA"[4] approach by the addition of other groups.

This swelling list included the Peoples Fedayeen, the Kurdish Democratic Party of Iran, Party for a free life in Kurdistan in 2009 and the Baluchi group Jundallah in 2010. Iran's nuclear ambitions are growing apace, since the restart of uranium enrichment activities in 2006, against all UN Security Council resolutions relating to non-proliferation and finding Iran in non-compliance, placed legally binding sanctions on Iran. In

---

[4] Cover Your Arse

2010, further legally binding sanctions were imposed, calling on Iran to halt its nuclear activities. During 2011, Iran was asked to engage with the IAEA[5] in talks to restore international confidence in the peaceful nature of its nuclear program.

The Iranian economy has been struggling as the result of the sanctions placed on it, obstacles still remain especially as Iran is seen to be the main sponsor of terrorism in the region and the US is deeply concerned as support grows for groups such as Hizbollah, Hamas and the Palestine Islamic Jihad, including Iran's support for the Assad regime in Syria and the Houthi rebels in Yemen. In 2015, the five permanent members of the UN Security Council plus Germany and the EU agreed that through a joint plan of action, Iran will have to allow the IAEA to verify key stages in that plan, prior to allowing the lifting of sanctions. Economic sanctions were lifted after the IAEA, certified that Iran had restricted its nuclear activities, but in 2017 the Iranian government test-fired a ballistic missile, the US placed immediate sanctions on Iran and in response, the Iranian government voted to invest heavily in a renewed ballistic missile programme. The US President Donald Trump described the 2015 nuclear deal the "worst ever", in Tehran as the result of the vote was given the Iranian parliament rang out to the words "death to America".

---

[5] International Atomic Energy Agency

US President Trump, during his campaign, made a promise to dismantle the nuclear deal but was warned by his Whitehouse staff that it would be counterproductive to do so. Iran is viewed by the US as providing advanced weapons in Yemen and in carrying out a proxy conflict against Saudi Arabia in the Red Sea.

Saudi Arabia

Saudi Arabia is situated in southwest Asia, it is the third largest country after China and India, it has a land mass in excess of seven hundred and fifty thousand square miles. The land is bordered by Jordon, Iraq, Kuwait, United Arab Emirates, Oman and Yemen.

Saudi Arabia and Kuwait agreed to divide the neutral zone between them, however, the maritime border with Iran is contested by all parties. The capital city is Riyadh, the land is also bounded by the Red Sea to the west and the Arabian Gulf to the east. One third is an area of sandy desert, the largest of which is two hundred and fifty thousand square miles, there are no lakes and no perennially running water.

As with most desert countries the climate is hot and very dry, where they regularly face dust and sand storms contrasted with very cold night-time temperatures. Agricultural land is in very short supply and natural vegetation is quite sparse. Wild animals abound such as Oryx, Jerboa, Lynx, Fox, Wildcat, Panther, Jackal, the favourite game bird is Bustard.

The human population is in excess of twenty-four million and ninety per cent are of common Arabian ancestry, Arabic is the native language with Semitic and Aramaic forming a small percentage, the business world including oil-related activities use

English. All citizens must be Muslim, the majority are Sunni, with Wahhabism as the dominant form, the remaining are Shia. There are no religious freedoms and the government controls all religious activities. The worshipping of non-Muslim faiths is prohibited and conversion from Islam to other faiths is a capital offence.

In 1932 various parts of the country joined to form the Kingdom of Saudi Arabia, the discovery of oil during the 1930s changed the countries fortunes as the reserves proved to be vast and a huge source of income, which expanded Saudi Arabia's influence in the world.

In 1973 Saudi Arabia became a key member of OPEC, it is the most moderate member altering oil flow to stabilize the International markets. From 1979 Islamic militants have been active and subsequently caused deep embarrassment to the monarchy, as they are credited with causing riots at the Grand Mosque. Iranian pilgrim riots during 1987 causing the suffocation of fourteen hundred, in 1997 three hundred killed by fire at a campsite and in 2004 a stampede during the Hajj with two hundred and fifty dead.

Saudi Arabian government does not recognise International Standards on Human Rights, the right to privacy, freedom of speech, assembly, religion and movement. Corporal punishment includes the amputation of limbs, beheading, stoning and executions are carried out for crimes which include, alcohol trafficking, armed robbery, adultery, and the practice of witchcraft, those who have been executed are mainly foreigners. Criticism of the fundamental principles of Islam and of basic government institutions, including the royal family, is not permitted and the government severely limits the freedom of speech punishing any dissent with detention and arrest.

Saudi Arabia's wealth and religious influence have been less than successful in its aim to counter Iranian influence in Iraq, nor in preventing Hizbollah taking power in Lebanon and the ongoing efforts and lack of progress on the Israeli-Palestinian peace process have come to nothing.

Saudi Arabia, Egypt, Bahrain and the United Arab Emirates, cut all ties with Qatar, as they claim that they accept terrorism and have a connection with Iran in the promotion of destabilising forces in the middle east. Qataris have been known to provide financial support to terrorist organisations such as Hamas. In a tit for tat response, Iran has accused Saudi Arabia of backing terrorism in Yemen, but it is the case that both Iran and Saudi Arabia support rival groups in Yemen, Syria, Iraq and Lebanon.

Saudi Arabian and Yemen al-Qa'eda merged to form al-Qa'eda in the Arab peninsular and based themselves in Yemen. The Yemeni army has launched offensives against Shia insurgents assisted by Saudi forces. The Shia rebels accused Saudi Arabia of providing support to Salafi groups in order that they can suppress Zaydis in Yemen.

In 2014, Iranian backed Houthi fighters took control of the Yemeni capital and proceeded to push towards Aden. In response Saudi Arabia led a coalition of Arab States, launching air and ground offensive campaign in 2015 to defeat the Shia fighters and to restore Yemen's government.

Turkey

The peninsula of the Anatolian plain with mountainous borderlands, this constitutes the main part of Turkey, it is a land that from its earliest history has been a battleground for warring factions. It consists of a high plateau which slopes down to the sea on three sides, in the south of the Mediterranean Sea, on the west Aegean Sea and in the north the Black Sea. The land mass is in excess of two hundred and ninety-seven thousand square miles, with a population in 2017, rising above eighty-one million, the majority are Turkish with the Kurds making up eighteen per cent and the remaining others seven per cent. The state official language is Turkish, with a minority Arabic and Kurdish, as for religion in 2017, the government states that ninety-nine per cent is Muslim with a minority of unaffiliated at thirteen per cent and Christian at two per cent. The main elements are sixty-five per cent Sunni and four per cent Shia, the country has a varied economy with a largely agricultural, industrial, electronic, manufacturing and defence sectors.

Turkey has a long history of expansionism and war with its neighbours, but over time its power had diminished, and by 1718 Hungary was lost, in 1774 the Crimea was annexed by Russia followed by Serbian independence in 1829 and full Greek independence in 1830. The rising power of Russia and Austria was a direct threat to Turkey, and fear of this led to Britain and France to support Turkey in the defeat of Russia during the Crimean War 1854-56 and again in the following Russian-Turkish war of 1877-78. Britain and Austria intervened and secured a revision of the treaty which Russia had dictated to Turkey, the Congress of Berlin in 1878 Bulgaria was made autonomous, Romania, Serbia and Montenegro were recognised as independent principalities which left the administration of Bosnia and Herzegovina under Turkish rule, this was given over to Austria, which was later annexed by Austria in 1908, and Bulgaria declared its complete independence in the same year.

Italy's seizure of Libya was recognised in 1912, Greece, Serbia, Bulgaria and Montenegro fought a war during 1912-13 which took from Turkey its European possessions. WWI completed the ruin of the Turkish empire when British forces in 1917-18 overran Iraq and Palestine which forced Turkey to sue for an armistice in 1918. Turkeys caliphate was abolished in 1924, they discarded its religious courts, Islam was no longer the state religion. The country was to be based on the system in Switzerland, which was adopted in 1924. The western calendar replaced the Islamic and the wearing of the Fez was forbidden in 1925, the use of Arabic was replaced by the Latin alphabet, women police officers were introduced in 1932, also polygamy and wearing of the veil were abolished. Latterly laws of 1934 required all Turks to adopt a surname, the adoption of the metric system of weights and measurements including the vote for women, all these changes inspired by Mustapha Kemal who later became known as Atatürk in 1934.

During WWII Turkey observed an armed neutrality, only declaring war on Germany and Japan in March 1945, in order that they would qualify for admission to the United Nations and the membership of NATO which followed in 1952.

The Armenian homeland remained under an Ottoman rule in WWI, Armenians living in their ancestral lands were systematically exterminated by the Ottoman Turks who allied themselves to the German Kaiser. The Armenians ruled what is now called Istanbul, these Christian Turks ruled from 30AD, making this the first nation to adopt Christianity.

Nationalists known as the young Turks over six months conducted a systematic uprooting and slaughter of some one million plus Armenians on the grounds they were infidels and racially inferior and traitors. The results of this carnage were recorded by Florence Nightingale and Clara Barton, as they carried out their field medical work. This resulted in the first genocide of the Twentieth Century, the reign of terror of Christian priests including the women and especially women, the breeding stock and unborn babies. The twenty-fourth of April in Armenia is known as Genocide Remembrance Day.

In 1915 the Turks had declared a temporary war of expropriation and the confiscation of property, land and livestock. All Armenian goods and chattels that had been seized were to be sold off. During 1918 the Turks carried out mass burnings of the population's villages, in a twisted form of gambling the sex of a child would be waged on and at the end they would disembowel the pregnant women and remove the child by skewering them on their bayonets. This was all carried out in the local church as a sacrilegious act, the intent was clear and no woman or child was safe. Eighty thousand Armenians from ninety villages across the Mus plain were burned in stables and haylofts, in Trabzon province fifty thousand children were overdosed with Morphine and two schools used as gas chambers. In coastal villages, they were not spared as women and children loaded into boats and later thrown overboard and left to drown, as this required immense effort it was changed to loading barges and having them capsized in the Black Sea. From all of these atrocities we can now see where the German state and Adolf Hitler and his cronies, got their ideas from and the roots of his final solution.

The current President of Turkey, Recep Tayyip Erodğan and his AKP[6] party are striving to replace Atatürk's secular society by an ideological and deliberate step to return to an Ottoman-style rule, creating an Islamic republic of what he termed a pious generation, which ISIS has not been able to achieve to date.

Erodğan's political economy and an Islamic resurgence in Turkey is a cause for concern, Turkish schools will in future teach the concept of Jihad, under the auspices of educational values, the government will provide new textbooks, which will be a huge blow to its secular education system. This new government-sponsored system will result in nothing less than their own children being brainwashed by embedding a Jihadist doctrine and with the potential to transform the middle east into a bloodbath.

Imam-Hatip high school will roll out courses on Jihad not as a religious war, but in the context of what the government described as a "loving nation". These draconian ideas include such things as women's obedience to men which will take the form of "worship", this type of doctrine is causing a backlash on social media in Turkey, such as no to a sexist curriculum and say no to non-scientific curriculum and defend secular education.

The government has displayed its means of rejection of unauthorised decent, which had a direct effect on the population and military resulting in the failed coup attempt by parts of the

---

[6] Adalet ve Kalkinma Partisi - Justice and Development Party

military. The World watched as Erodğan's government removed not just the military ringleaders, but tens of thousands of civilians from public posts, as they are deemed subversive, but most likely not from the party faithful.

Turkey began playing a role which was well rehearsed in Pakistan and Afghanistan in support of the US in Syria. During this time Turkey has relaunched its war on its Kurdish population in the southeast of the country, this proved to be disastrous enterprise possibly providing the trigger for the coup attempt in 2016.

Kurds PKK[7] fighting for autonomy or independence oppressed by the Turkish government because of their ethnicity and cultural identity, Erodğan's views this issue as a terrorist problem and is looking to forcibly move the Kurds out of Turkey and into northern Iraq. This, in turn, is fuelling radicalisation among the Turk-Kurd population, which is reminiscent of the Armenian genocide from 1915, the Turkish state under Erodğan has cleared parts of the country with whole Kurdish districts empty of their population.

Turkey, Russia and Iran have set in place a de-escalation process which Turkey is playing to its advantage, military equipment such as tanks, artillery and APC's[8] crossed the

---

[7] Partiya Karkerên Kurdistan - Kurdistan Workers Party
[8] Armoured Personnel Carrier

Turkish border from Killis into Syria and deployed these assets in Azaz, Marea and Tel Rifaat, with bases at Marea, Tunais, Kel Jibril during Euphrates Shield. Turkey controlled groups in Syria fight each other west of the Euphrates river, the solution was to turn these groups attention on fighting the Kurdish group the YPG.[9] The PYD[10] and YPG are US-backed forces and Turkey will not allow these Kurdish groups create a Kurd state in northern Syria, Turkey says the PYD is an offshoot of the PKK and are viewed by them as a terrorist organisation. As Turkey tried to turn towards Manbij when the US hoisted its flag the Turkish forces conceded, as America and Russia are a part of the Astana-agreement for protecting Manbij. Turkey then focused their efforts on Afrin only to discover that Russia had sent a mission in the guise of mounting a cease-fire.

Turkey deployed troops on the ground to enforce the agreement but did not include the main rebel groups in Ilib, such as al-Qaeda offshoot Tahrir al-Sham or what was formerly known as the Nusra Front. It is massing tanks on the border with Syria and going after non-Jihadi factions which are collectively known as the Free Syrian Army which includes the Kurds, this is to prevent a Kurdish corridor or self-rule.

---

[9] Yekineyên Parastina Gel - Peoples Protection Units
[10] Partiya Yekitiya Demokrat - Democratic Union Party

US troops patrol the Turkey-Syria border after Turkish airstrikes on the Kurds, these airstrikes targeting Sinjar mountains in northern Iraq, leaving the US as deeply concerned for what the US sees as bombing its allies in countering ISIS. The Turks have made it clear they will not entertain anything that looks anything near a Kurdish state and sees this issue as its own business.

Turkey has taken steps to normalise its relationship with Russia and Iran and mend fences with Assad's most important ally, who would then be expected to turn a blind eye and either give a green light or look the other way to Turkey's intervention in northern Syria, as it feels threatened by Kurdish territorial ambitions and as the relationship has soured between the Syrian Kurds and Assad's government. Assad's problem is the US and it is quite likely at some point that war will break out, as the US military has scrambled fighter jets to deter the Syrian military from bombing the Kurds.

Turkey is likely to face a backlash from NATO member states as it proceeds with closer ties with Russia and Iran, NATO could be faced with having a member state providing a running commentary via the back door as to NATOs intentions, or face the possibility of a member being classed as a failed state, this would leave only two possibilities either Turkey leaves, or be expelled.

President Recep Tayyip Erodğan won a historic referendum that granted him new powers and his leadership extended till 2029, he has banned Wikipedia, matchmaking shows on TV, fired four thousand more civil servants, with an authoritative stance to freedom of information, opposition figures have been arrested and continues the purge in the aftermath of the failed coup. Turkey has moved from a parliamentary system to a power executive presidency with unchecked powers and heading towards dictatorship.

Pakistan

Pakistan was created on the fifteenth of August 1947 by annexation from India by the British, prior to that date it formed part of British India and over many centuries there have been many clashes of culture between Hindus and Muslim populations.

It was said that "no one man can be designated as the father of Pakistan", Syed Ahmed Kahn 1817-98, he believed that a revival of Muslim power was possible through the absorption of western ideas and friendship with Britain. The actual architect of Pakistan was Mahomed Ali Jinnah 1867-1948, he was for many years the President of the Muslim League.

Lord Mountbatten was sent to Deli as Viceroy to affect a settlement, between Hindus and Muslim's as fierce clashes between the two had ensued. Mountbatten who had been given full powers to resolve the political deadlock, did so with such dramatic quickness that large sections of the population were caught unawares, with millions of Muslim's and Hindus pouring over the frontiers during the months following, the Hindu population would remain in India, while Pakistan would contain mostly Muslim's, this resulted in mass riots and the rape of countless women solely due to the lack of law and order while political unrest raged out of control. It has been estimated that up to two million people lost their lives in the wake of the split, all down to the political ineptitude of Mountbatten.

Democracy was stalled by martial law due to a number of cross-border wars with India. After adopting a presidential system in 1962, the country had experienced good economic growth when in 1965 Pakistan suffered an economic downturn due to a second war with India. In 1970 Pakistan saw its first democratic elections since independence, a move to take back control from military rule, but after the military establishment refused to hand over power in East Pakistan, this act delayed democratic rule which did not resume until 1972, this was predictably short-lived as it ended by another military coup in 1977. Since then there has been further political turmoil with a number of bloodless coups between Musharraf and Benazir Bhutto, until her assassination in 2007. The general election in 2013 saw Nawaz Sharif elected as Prime Minister.

Pakistani involvement in the war on terror cost one-hundred and eighteen billion US dollars, the wars in neighbouring Afghanistan during the 1980's and 1990's forced millions of Afghan refugees into Pakistan, who settled mainly in the tribal areas. Pakistan, Iran and China are collectively trying to slice up Afghanistan, firstly by supporting the Mujahideen and the Pakistani Taliban, who rely heavily on the Pakistani ISI,[11] who supported rebels such as Gulbuddin Hekmatyar, Ashamed Shah Masoud, and the Haqqani Network in targeting a very weak Afghan government.

Since 1994 Pakistan has tried to destabilise the political process in Afghanistan, from the Taliban capture of Kandahar in the same year and after the subsequent death of Osama bin Laden, prominent Afghan figures have been assassinated by the Haqqani's who are directly linked to the Pakistan Government. In 2017 Kabul attack, Pakistan instigated an "undeclared war of aggression" on Afghanistan which is facing a war on all fronts, the most serious of which is the systematic interference by Pakistan and Iran who claim access over Afghan water resources.

Pakistan and Iran have been involved in sabotage, murder and meddling in the implementation of the Salma Dam, Iranian guards on the border have opened fire on Afghan residents while collecting drinking water from the Hari Rud River in Afghanistan, while there is a history of hijack and diplomatic meddling in the investment by donor countries in the Afghan hydro project.

Pakistan has the second largest number of Muslim's in the world after Indonesia, the majority are Sunni. Pakistan helped the independence movements of Indonesia, Algeria, Tunisia, Morocco and Eritrea.

---

[11] Pakistan ISI: Inter-Services Intelligence

Chapter 3
Asia Pacific

Southeast Asia

Indonesia a Muslim majority country has Malaysia, the Philippines to the north and Papua New Guinea to the east with Australian Northern Territories to the south, surrounded by the Indian and Pacific oceans.

Its capital is Jakarta with a population in excess of two-hundred and sixty-million people, eighty-seven per cent Muslim, the country has an abundance of natural resources in oil, gas, tin, copper, gold and agriculture of rice, palm oil, tea, coffee, medicinal plants and rubber, it is classed as a megadiverse[12] country. The earliest known inhabitants were Homo erectus "Java Man", Indonesia is made up of over thirteen-thousand islands.

Malaysia capital is Kuala Lumpur with a population in excess of thirty-one million, sixty-three percent Muslim. Islam is the state religion and is made up of thirteen states and three federal territories. The country has a new market economy with abundant natural resources oil, tin, rubber, palm oil and its own space programme and it is classed as a megadiverse country.

Philippines capital is Manila with a population in excess of one-hundred million, Islam is the second highest religion at

---

[12] A group of nations that harbour the majority of Earth species

eleven per cent, it is made up of and in excess of seven-thousand islands and is classed as a megadiverse country. It has abundant natural resources in copper, oil, coconut oil and fruits also a manufacturer of semiconductors.

Papua New Guinea capital is Port Moresby with a population around eight-million with one per cent Muslim. It has mineral deposits of gold, oil and copper its agriculture includes palm oil, coffee, coconut oil, tea and rubber and is classed as a megadiverse country.

Australia's capital is Canberra it has a population of in excess of twenty-four million and a land mass which is over thirty-one times that of the UK. The population per square kilometre is just under three and in the UK, it is over two-hundred and forty-eight. It has a large market economy and a high GDP,[13] rich in natural resources with agriculture in beef, sheep, wool and wine, minerals are iron-ore, gold, liquified natural gas and coal and is classed as a megadiverse country. It's population of the Muslim faith is two-point six per cent.

These five countries have been identified by Islamic terrorists as the next countries to come under Islamic control and to form an Islamic Caliphate. A large indigenous Muslim population which would prove easy to overpower the smaller non-Muslim populations and to gain control of what are very rich

---

[13] Gross Domestic Product 1.31 trillion US Dollars

countries. Katibah Nusantara the Southeast Asia wing of ISIS formed from Malaysian and Indonesian fighters in Syria since the mid 2014's. Al-Ma'unah group or ISIS in the Pacific, an al-Qa'eda linked splinter group Jemaah Islamiyah and indigenous jihadi groups built on Afghanistan veterans will provide the core of the operation. Islamic politics in two Muslim majority countries in Southeast Asia, Indonesia and Malaysia, this area of the Pacific has emerged as a second front in the US war on terror. As security concerns over Islamic radicalization and the Talibanization of Indonesia and Malaysia, where can be found terror cells Jemaah Islamiyah and al-Qa'eda funded by Wahabi money and ideology.

Organised forces of Islamic radicalism will focus on matters such as pro-Shari'ah resurgence to lay the groundwork in establishing an Islamic State. Plural forms of Islam have been challenged by fundamentalist tendencies with a battle of ideas between moderates and radicals within Muslim communities.

Iran, Libya and Saudi Arabia confer exceptionalism on Asian Pacific Islam to account for the rise in abnormal radical tendencies, Indonesian and Malaysian consequences for Islam is a point of comparison and the examination of the significance of state-centred religious authority for Islamic politics and the ideological identification of the state with Muslim interests. Wahabi inspired activists having links with individuals in Saudi

Arabia and the tensions between Islamic ideals and nationhood in Indonesia gives them levers for ISIS activity.

Clashes between economic management and the political administration have resulted in small underground groups resorting to terror, who are hell-bent on establishing an Islamic state through violence. Malaysian Islamic Youth Movement, a shadowy group which the government claimed were pursuing the Darul Islam dream of an Islamic state had emerged from a mosque where sermons allegedly combined with anti-government agitation. Islamists explain their actions as applying Gods law called "shahid" holly bombing, suicide bombing is considered a heroic act of martyrdom, a selfless sacrifice in the service of God and religion. It is justified in a state of war to rescue Muslims!

Katibah Nusantara a dedicated Southeast Asian unit within ISIS it has a strategy of waging global jihad. While Malaysian speaking jihadists who fought in Afghanistan formed the backbone of Jemaah Islamiyah. Katibah Nusantara first major combat success was by capturing Kurd-held territories in Syria in 2015, this success was highlighted on Islamic social media especially in Indonesia and Malayan languages to entice new recruits. The strategic goal of establishing a worldwide caliphate and to undertake attacks in Southeast Asia and by playing a part in connecting local extremist networks. Most of the leaders include Indonesians and Malayans which was formed in 2014 and headquartered in Syria.

ISIS is an organisation that was built on a narrow and dogmatic interpretation of Islam that the Malaysian and Indonesian governments have allowed to develop over decades. In the case of Indonesia some Islamic groups as the Mujahideen of eastern Indonesia, have been peacefully promoting radical ideologies to the Muslim majority where-by parts of the Muslim population without joining the organization formerly, may be embracing the Wahabi ideology.

The threat from Jemaah Islamiyah and other Salafi jihadist groups remain undiminished and encompasses Indonesia, Malaysia, Singapore, the Philippines and Australia. A breakaway faction of Darul Islam was responsible for a series of bombings 2002 Bali, 2004 Australia embassy, likewise "KOMPAK"[14] a violent faction of an Islamic charity of the same name now forms part of Jemaah Islamiyah, which the former head established Jemaah Ansharut Tauhid, as an above ground jihadist group, who publishes a magazine and does public outreach to spread Salafi-jihadist ideas, they also have a paramilitary wing which conducts training exercises for the willing.

---

[14] Mujahidin, Darul Islam in Indonesia Sulawesi province "the crisis management/prevention committee"

Southeast Asia is fast becoming al-Qa'eda's second front, with global Salafi-jihadist ideas and goals, the establishment of an Islamic state in an Indonesian pro-caliphate. In 2012 the face of violent extremism in Indonesia had changed yet again, targets have shifted away from large-scale bombings to targeted assassinations and small-scale bombings often directed at the police and mosques. Prison is a venue for radicalization as jihadist leaders have been allowed to hold study circles by prison officials. Many of the prisons allow senior hardcore jihadists to mix with what is termed as "followers" including criminals which provide a host of informal interactions allowing radicalizations to occur.

Papua New Guinea and Australia are in the crosshairs of the Islamic state for very different reasons, Papua has only a small population which can easily be overcome over time as the Muslim population increases, this would place a strain on the local population and government. An ungoverned region between the Sulu Sea, Sabah and Sulawesi Sea, where ease of passage for militants and terrorists including arms trafficking by Jemaah Islamiyah. Australia could face the same outcome, but on the other hand due to the size of the country Muslim enclaves are more likely to be set up. The purchase of whole estates over time would give calls for mosques and Muslim community centres to be built, with Arabic street names following these acquisitions these estates would grow into small towns which are again given Arabic names, once this occurs the likely rise of Islamic community councils then as they vote in Shari'ah law, bobs your uncle you have a caliphate, a country within a country, a government within a government.

Australia may have a points-based immigration system which is fine, but this has been sidestepped over recent times, immigrant holding centres have been closed down due to the backlash from Australian citizens who felt that this was inhumane treatment. This has led to violence on the streets of towns and cities, not always a Muslim problem but African-descent youths forming gangs and going on the rampage which they see as a normal activity, as imported from their mother country. Australia in 2016 is faced with a new breed of jihadist, social outcasts with a history of mental illness, vulnerable and easily radicalized lone-wolves. The government's anti-terrorist agencies have disrupted nine planned terrorist attacks since 2014, faced with lone-wolf attackers who are rapidly radicalized including through Muslim community outreach.

In 2017 Australia is seeing strains of Islamic terrorism in the Indo-Pacific region, ISIS sympathizers are attempting to kidnap the Malay political leadership, they have also found a fertile climate for a rise in popularity, a far cry from a once religious conservative moderate government led country.

Malaysia is now a heavily politicized country with the dominant party, Malay-Muslim who promote Muslim dominance and supremacy. They allow right-wing religious groups to preach jihad against the enemies of Islam the Christians and Hindus with blatant state-sanctioned Friday prayers propaganda.

Pro-ISIS and pro-Jemaah Islamiyah, jihadi ideologies from radical clerics such as Abu Bakar Ba'asyir and Aman Abdurrahman chief ISIS ideology in Indonesia who swore allegiance to ISIS in 2014 only to renounce this later, so that they could take advantage of bringing their radical ideas and sermons to the fore, as they have enjoyed ready access to a disaffected audience whilst in prison.

The jihadists will not give up and go away, they will continue to work towards their goals. Australia has a very long coastline and it is practically impossible to defend it against small-scale jihadi cells, who have a myriad of small islands to cross into Australian territory and once there, they have a large land mass to choose from.

Chapter 4

The Dark Side of Islam

The legality of jihad is viewed as typical of radical Islamic ideology, it is the basis for actual behaviour and on the basis of legal interpretation. Conservative moderate's beliefs in traditional Islamic jurisprudence "shari'ah" with a ruling "fatwa", by authoritative Islamic scholars.

Muslim activists quote verses from the Meccan Period appear for love, peace and patience which are then nullified by the Medina Period, abrogated and rendered void by later passages that incite killing, decapitations, maiming, terrorism and religious intolerance.

How does this come about I hear you ask? In every Mosque alongside the Qur'an can be found a four-book volume, a manual printed and supplied by radical institutions which the majority of Muslims are schooled in, the book is on Shari'ah law called Sahih al-Bukhari. This book is printed in Arabic so that non-speakers would not be able to translate it but they offer up a book which is heavily abridged from the four-book volume, either in English or another language, it is what they want you to know, and that you should not know all.

The following paragraphs have been sourced from an English interpretation of Islamic verses by the Australian Imam Tawhidi;

The Sahih al-Bukhari is source material for the Grand Ayatollahs so they can interpret the Qur'an for all Muslims as there are seventy-three dominations of Islam. So just what is it that needs interpreting, the radical ideology that Muslims around the world riot and kill people because they think the prophet Mohammed has been insulted, the following is taken from book 2. "Mohammed was sent to Earth so he can have intimate relations with eleven wives a day and night twenty-four seven", therefore Islamic men are trying to emulate the prophet. Islamic youth believe that they will receive seventy-two vestal virgins, "mother to your life and lifestyle", says Imam Tawhidi.

Prophet Mohammed says, book 2-chapter 6 segment 7 – page 223,

"Vow by God, that I wish I could be killed for the sake of Allah, then brought back to life, then killed, then brought back to life, then killed, then brought back to life, then be killed once again to become a Martyr."

This book is responsible for the non-stop attacks towards the West and is the route for terrorism, and radicalization of the young into suicide bombing to please the prophet in loving Martyrdom.

Book 2-chapter 59 – segment 11 page 348,

The characteristics of Satan and his soldiers.

The wife of Mohammed, Iesha killed ten thousand people when she led an army at the "battle of the Camel", Iesha aged between six to thirteen-years-old, a wife who conceived a child prior to her marriage to the prophet. She says the prophet Mohammed was possessed, he was a crazy delusional man to the extent that he would imagine things, delusional in that he would delude in himself, that he had done things or been responsible for things he had not actually done. In this book ninety-five per cent of the Islamic faith believe in this book which says Mohammed is a psychopath and possessed, interpreted by Imam Tawhidi.

Book 2-chapter 59 – page 377,

Qur'an, do not differentiate between prophets.

Prophet Mohammed would doubt previous prophets, which clearly contradicts the Holy Qur'an, Mohammed states that Muslims are worthier than Abraham.

Book 3-segment 44 – Hadith – page 462,

Mohammed says, "whoever wakes up and eats dates (whether be same or different) will be immune to poisoning during that day".

Book 4-chapter – Medicine with the Urine of the Camel – page 16,

A group of people came and visited the Medina, where the prophet had his religion established and they became sick, as the prophet was the best doctor, Mohammed he ordered them, that they go after the owner of the camel, to drink from its milk and urine, until their bodies become strong again, they killed the owner of the camel and stole the camel. They came back, "bring to me those who did this to the owner of the camel", so they brought them, Mohammed chopped their hands off and their legs for stealing the camel and poked their eyes out with two nails.

Fathers cannot sit in the presence of their daughters without having the mother present. Wahabi men are raised to perv at every lady, therefore fathers perv at their daughters, touching them, hugging them for too long, which has been reported and sleeping beside their daughters in a sexual manner. Religious fundamentalist spiritual satisfaction where intimacy is the main goal, (people should not believe in any god where a sexual reward is on offer).

Shari'ah law number twelve, women are prohibited from eating bananas, carrots, or cucumbers without first chopping them up, or otherwise treated as a phallic sexual act.

It's not permissible to engage in sexual intercourse and sexual penetration with a wife before nine years of age, but from nine years onwards you can, whether it is a permanent or temporary marriage. As for other sexual pleasures, touching her sexually, hugging her sexually, stripping her of her clothing and laying her on her back against her will, hold her thighs together and penetrate her thighs "thighing" even if a new-born baby.

If he penetrates the girl before she is nine, but does not take her virginity, then nothing will happen to this man other than he has sinned and that is between himself and god. Therefore, there is no fine or imprisonment, no accountability and no punishment for molesting a child. If he penetrates a young baby, rips the young baby so that the private parts are damaged, if he rapes the girl we will tell him to stop, then in this case, he can no longer penetrate. A new born baby or young baby has been defiled or raped, should the mother divorce then the child is likely to be raped several times and made to bleed as a fine.

Fat female baby girls are able to endure sexual intercourse because she is fat, as a skinny toddler will die. A subject which is taught in Islamic schools, that it is ok to penetrate and engage in sexual intercourse even if the baby is incapable of intercourse because the little baby is the wife of an elderly man and he has rights. The little baby needs to give rights to a man, she needs to give sex to a man and if she does not then he rapes her. Breast fed babies are included, if the parents of the young baby and that baby is under the age of nine years, agree that the little girl should have sex with her husband then there is no problem with that.

Shari´ah law, Mohammed's words are "hadith" his actions are "sunnah" and the Qur'an is the interpretation of Shari´ah law called "fiqh" by muftis.[15] Shari´ah law regulates public, private behaviour and private beliefs, it prioritizes punishment over rehabilitation with penalties that favour corporal, capital punishments over incarceration and is the most intrusive laws focused on women.

Published and taught in Iran, you are not to use high-speed internet, to smoke is illegal, to eat fast food or use air-conditioning in public, anyone who does this is a sinner. It is illegal to give roses as the scent arouses passions, it is illegal to speak English, wear a hat, and for females to drive.

Shari´ah law court rulings include criticism of Allah, Mohammed and the Quran and are punishable by death, likewise, a Muslim who becomes a non-Muslim, also non-Muslims who marries a Muslim or leads a Muslim away from their faith will also be punished by death interpreted by Imam Tawhidi.

As for women;

Testimonies from four male witnesses are required to prove rape of a female Q24:13

A woman who alleges rape without producing four male witnesses is guilty of adultery.

A woman found guilty of adultery is punished by death.

---

[15] Jurist who interprets Shari'ah Law.

A male convicted of rape can have his conviction dismissed by marrying his victim.

Muslim men have sexual rights to any woman not wearing a Hijab.

A woman can have one husband, but a husband can have up to four wives.

A man can marry an infant girl and consummate the marriage when she is nine years old.

Girls clitoris should be cut Hadith 5251

A man can beat his wife for insubordination Q4:34

A man can divorce his wife, but a wife needs her husband's consent to divorce.

A divorced wife loses custody of all children over six years old, or when they reach this age.

A woman's testimony in court, allowed only in property cases, carries half the weighting of a man.

A female heir inherits half of that of a male heir.

A woman cannot speak to a man who is not her husband or relative.

It's not surprising that Muslim women are not taught English in the UK, otherwise they would be able to understand what is going on around them, being unable or discouraged from learning keeps females close to their community and where their husbands can exercise control to what they are allowed to hear and how they should act and more importantly how they should vote. This is vote rigging is tantamount to rigging an election, which is a criminal act.

Wahhabism sometimes referred to as Salafiyya avoids western dress, neckties, laughter, the western form of salutation such as handshakes, applause, discouraging sporting activities. Islamic fundamentalism is the belief in reopening of the gates of ijtihad "independent reasoning".

Fundamentalists are primarily interested in revolution, less interested in modernity and less willing to associate with non-Muslims. Islamists and fundamentalists are committed to Shari´ah law, Islamists generally tend to favour the education of women while the fundamentalists preach for women to return to the home, Islamists believe it is sufficient that sexes be separated in public.

Fundamentalists fatwahs such as "every Muslim who pleads for the suspension of the Shari´ah is an apostate and can be killed. These killings cannot be prosecuted under Islamic law because the killing is justified". The Muslim world against the infidels with the restoration of the Caliphate, reviving the concept of jihad to evict an infidel from a Muslim country as a personal duty. Jihad is an act of faith in Allah and "why do you cling to this world when the next world is better" ideology in which death is idealized as a desired goal and not a necessary evil in war.

Islamic marital jurisprudence, a Muslim slaveholder is entitled by law to the sexual enjoyment of his slave women and that the property of a slave is owned by their master. Islam permits sexual relations between a male master and his female slave outside marriage "ma Malak at aymanukum" what your right hand possesses. There is no limit on the number of concubines a master may possess, female slaves in many Muslim societies were prey for their owner's household, their neighbours and their guests, as slavery is ingrained in the structural increase of importing slaves from non-Muslim countries. Slavery was also perceived as a means of converting non-Muslim's to Islam, morally as well as physically the slave is regarded in law as an inferior being and as both a person and a possession.

The supreme leader of Iran declares the permissibility of slavery in modern times, "today if there is a war between Muslims and the infidels, we will take slaves, the ruling on slavery has not expired and is eternal and we will bring them to the world of Islam. Slavery is a part of Islam, slavery is a part of Jihad and Jihad will remain as long as there is Islam".

Madrassahs are Islamic religious schools which have built extremely close ties with radical militant groups and play a critical role in sustaining the international terrorist network. They no longer focus on producing the next generation of religious scholars and clerics, but now dominate the education system as a whole. The primary danger of this is the increased number and influence is that many of the more radical schools have become havens for extremist groups that teach militancy contrary to the tenets of Islam. They provide a yearly supply of recruits to violent fundamentalists.

Abigail Haworth reporting for The Observer in 2012 while in Indonesia looking into female genital mutilation, reported that the reasons for this practice were described as "it balances their emotions so that women and girls don't get sexually over-stimulated" also "it helps them to urinate more easily and reduce the bad smell". She interviewed a twelve-year-old girl who was the oldest of 248 girls, the youngest being five-months in a mass ceremony, an event on the prophet Mohammed's birthday. The twelve-year-old told her "I was shaking and crying last night, I was so scared I could not sleep" later she retorted that it was "a very bad sharp pain", she stated that "we will have a special meal at home then read the Qur'an and later I will listen to my Britney Spears CD".

A female doctor gynaecologist from an Islamic hospital gave an interview and stated that "you can have it done here if you wish, but I don't recommend it. It's not mandatory in Islam and it is painful!". FGM is an ancient cultural practice that existed prior to Islam and for the majority of the world the practice is seen as barbaric, but for Islamic countries, this practice has become the norm.

In Britain, Muslims are not allowed to take British Citizenship, if this is by right of birth, they must renounce it in the name of Islam.

Chapter 5
Your Inner Jihadi

Young people today spend more of their time online than ever before, since the advent of the internet providing easy access to social media. This is proving a breeding ground for recruits looking for those who are vulnerable, not necessarily socially inept, but who tend to be averse to social contact within their community. Spending long hours each day trawling through whatever they fancy, texting whoever and up or downloading images from YouTube, mostly in their most private space.

In these circumstances, an individual will interact with what is described as fake news and the unwary can fall foul to the validity of such news items, or fake photoshop images. Internet propaganda can lead to early engagement with violent ideologies, it is extremely easy to view extremist material and allow access to online communities that support violent ideologies.

Making contact with likeminded individuals can move to a stage where physical contact can take place, either through sports clubs or religious study groups or any other type of social congregation. Under these circumstances, individuals can become vulnerable to selection and subsequent moral change.

Group selection can occur where an individual is found to be sensitive to their influence and radicalisation can begin, in the first instance by recruiters or authority figures then by peer pressure. Radicalisation and Deradicalization follow very similar routes although the outcomes are quite different, they both follow tried and tested behaviour therapy.

Psychodynamic and Humanistic therapy approaches use classical conditioning principles to change behaviour. Behavioural modification can be achieved through positive reinforcement, operant conditioning and cognitive behaviour therapy. Learning based treatment methods in order to effect change in the way someone thinks as well as acts, is a product of past experience. The teacher or trainer helps to replace undesirable thoughts, to create change, for good or ill, to bring about systematic change and cognitive restructuring.

Assertiveness training is usually conducted within a group along with psychological modelling to create the desired behaviours, this is backed by peer pressure using positive reinforcement to effect a change in behaviour patterns. Collectively a group will repeat phrases and copy actions rather akin to military recruits learning to march and keep in step.

Deindividuation is where an individual becomes engulfed by a group and where they lose their sense of individuality, allowing them to experience emotional arousement, therefore reinforce prejudice and discrimination and promote changes in behaviour, so to carry out acts that they previously would not otherwise do alone. Another useful tool in modifying behaviour is through conformity and compliance, individuals do not always conform to social influence where ambiguity or uncertainty will determine physical reality.

The more uncertain reality becomes the more likely an individual will seek and rely on others opinions, which focuses group conformity no matter how delusional.

Inducing compliance to change what you say, what you do, on request and asking for the individual or group to agree to a small request, then asking for ever larger ones. The results of all these methods is the desired response of obedience, a change in behaviour and to a demand from an authoritative figure.

Milgram's experiment in 1963 is a good example, in this experiment a subject was strapped into a chair, electrodes were fastened to his wrists and the experiment participants were told that if the subject got an answer wrong to a question, they were to press a button and the subject would receive an electric shock. The participants were told that after each time the button was pressed the electric shock voltage would increase, luckily the subject would not receive an electric shock, but the participants did not know this.

The experiment went something like this, after the first shock it all went quiet, the supervisor of the experiment told the participant to increase the voltage, at each incorrect answer and subsequent depression of the button there were cry's, later incorrect answers resulted in screams, which got louder and louder on each occasion the button was pressed. Each time the supervisor asked to increase the voltage none of the participants refused to comply, even though the lower voltages were strong enough to kill. Participants who raised concerns still complied with the supervisor's request, when the supervisor only had to tell them it was "its ok, nothing to worry about!".

The use of violent video games on social media can play an important role, social media characters are seen as social beings, this type of play stimulates the same brain activity as it would in real life aggression. Virtual violence can result in user behaviour following the intention to do harm. There is a perception of reality and as the game progresses, they are led into emotional detachment, this also offers pleasurable gratifications and proof of their own superiority, making them feel effective and powerful, coupled with the loss of moral concern and disengagement.

What motivates some individuals to terrorist organisations and how is it that these organisations are able to radicalize these individuals. The answer lies in natural human behaviours, a desire for external rewards and attain internal satisfaction. Our behaviour is driven by the desire for esteem from others, approval, admiration and personal achievement.

How we perceive our personal identity in our area of origin, what ethnic group, clan or religious kinship, can provide a rite of passage and perceived power in a community. Social boundaries relate to the way in which the individual sees themselves and others. Dissociating those who are reviled and degraded or otherwise undesirable, this reinforces their own righteousness, which can become a positive political or terrorist act in other words two sides of the same coin. In these actions, it all depends on individual skills and the tendency to learn from the actions of others.

Emotions rely on a number of actors, the need to feel part of something, feel the need for enduring relationships, or religious belief. These emotions are generated by the brain, and are hard-wired, unless there is a problem with brain function the emotions will be unchanged. Should there be a problem with brain function, emotions can be changed by producing unconscious acts, a loss of control, which could lead to murder. Studies in murders have shown brain damage and dysfunction in the frontal lobe with a resultant loss of control of their impulses.

"Psychopath" is now commonly called ant-social personality disorder, which has been identified as a malfunction of the brain, the result of which is having little or no response to another's distress and are also immune to the feelings of guilt or pangs of conscience. Public welfare and safety is the most serious and costly public concern, anti-social personality disorder has a long-term pattern of irresponsibility, impulsive, unscrupulous and even criminal behaviour, beginning in childhood or early adolescence. Sufferers can be charming, intelligent and at the same time be self-centred manipulators. Some research suggests this has a genetic predisposition which makes it difficult to alter their behaviour, strangely these individuals become less active from the age of forty.

There is no deterrence for psychopaths as the pleasure and feelings of accomplishment in carrying out violence overwhelm "I just wanted to know what it would be like to kill somebody" even though they had killed before but felt that this earlier act was too long ago. They know people get hurt but do not think they have to go that far, but see them as an obstacle, people are run by others feelings and emotions "why care, you cannot look at everybody as a person, or you would never do anything as feelings get in the way and stop everything".

A conflict-filled childhood can produce the foundation for the psychological and social development of ant-social personality disorder, other factors include child abuse, poverty and other environmental conditions can produce high arousal levels leading to sensation seeking and impulsivity.

Moral development is lacking as a direct result of the lack of parental guidance and reasoning. Obedience to those who portray authority in order to avoid punishment, while pleasing others to get their approval and above all seen to be following the rules. Displaying what looks like high moral reasoning is no guarantee to act morally, this can lead to incorrect perception on the part of society, this usually is described by observers as "this is out of character" or "quiet, never bothered anybody".

Other disorders although quite relatively rare, are dissociative, which can lead to a sudden loss of memory and the adoption of a new identity, some far east countries report individuals being possessed by a religious god. For some sufferers, they can have multiple identities, each of which speaks, acts and writes in a different way and this is commonly called, multiple personality disorder.

An after-school Madrasa called the "lantern of knowledge" a terrorist teacher at an Islamic primary school used role play "stabbing police officers", Umar Ahmed Haque aged twenty-five an unqualified teacher. He tried to radicalize children by employing role-playing techniques during after school classes, Abuthaher Mamun aged twenty-nine and Mohammed Abid aged twenty-seven were also involved in teaching up to two hundred and fifty youngsters at two east end London schools and the Ripple Road Mosque. Fifty-five children between the ages of eleven and fourteen told police they would be murdered if they revealed the content of his lessons. These dangerous individuals were trying to create an army of children to attack with guns, knives, bombs, and cars to kill innocent people, all of these methods are well tried and tested on the war on terror in Afghanistan and Iraq as children can get close to ground troops.

Clinical explanations to identify a unique terrorist profile, the relationship between psychopathology and terrorism, that mental illness and abnormality are typically not critical factors in terrorist behaviour and would rarely be considered classic psychopaths, but terrorism is a complex and dynamic process. People come to adopt violent extremist ideologies and engage in violent actions through stages such as, an individual becomes receptive to the possibility of new ideas and worldviews or, seeks meaning through a religious idiom or, experiences religious lessons and activities that facilitate indoctrination and identity construction.

The radicalization process comprises of four main stages, pre-radicalization, conversion, indoctrination and action. Ideologies support terrorism which in turn provides a set of beliefs that guide and justify which cannot be questionable nor be questioned, all behaviours are goal orientated and are seen as serving the cause. To this end its "us or them", supported by a sacred authority which continues to reinforce that "us" is at risk from "them" as "us" is seen as being good and right which promotes internal cohesion and strengthens external opposition and to impel direct action.

Moral disengagement resulting in dehumanization which erodes social justice as violence becomes justified and as a group justification for extremist violence. An elevation of intolerance through the demonizing of opponents or civil government is seen as illegitimate, with anticipation of supernatural intervention and the glorification of "dying for the cause" with the promise of a future paradise.

Terrorist recruitment using "join the Jihad" through friendship and kinship, they operate as "rational prospectors", they seek to identify those most likely to agree to act, also to use information in finding likely recruits and offer participatory opportunities and employ inducements to say "yes". Radicalization through mobilization is the direction of activity with the focus on the cause and those who oppose it, the critical factors in mobilization are through a sense of belonging, personal meaning and the approval of "God". The psychological costs can be reduced by deindividualization, obedience, the individual's inhibition or restraint by reducing self-awareness while facilitating conformity.

Moral disengagement through the breaking down the barriers by group ideology, usually described as the "group think", in this case blaming the victim for deserving retribution. Terrorist groups must maintain cohesion and loyalty to its collective belief system in order to deter dissent and maintain its "drumbeat" to fight boredom and inactivity, manage group identity and manipulate incentives in keeping a focus on group objectives and their motivation to act. Profile of perpetrators includes the far-right or far-left, ethnocentric youths, criminal youths and fellow travellers, misfits and drifters. Commonly they do not join an extremist group because they hold extremist views but adopt extremist views because they have become involved with an extremist group in the search of "action and excitement" or a political or religious duty. They tend to embrace Jihadism or other forms of militancy through a combination of loyalty to the leader and political activism, often intelligent but impressionable and easily manipulated by the elders they look up to, for some the experience of belonging and being accepted by peers, they seek friendship, comradeship, protection and fulfilment of social needs.

Radicals have used methods similar to the one's paedophiles employ when grooming children to softly win over their targets, giving chocolates and items of clothing to impressionable young men and women.

Chapter 6
Life in a Caliphate

Dar al-Islam "The House of Islam", re-Islamization of Muslim society and the restoration of an Islamic government based on shari'ah, a jihad offensive against the infidels and the restoration of the caliphate.

What the "fatwa"? Saudi cleric Salih al Munajid calls for a fatwa ruling to kill Mickey Mouse, Tom and Jerry, watch out Disneyland as children are at risk from dressing up as these characters. Radical Islam ideology of sex for killing, sex and money and a cooked dinner in a restaurant with Mohammed. Jihadi sex "girls join ISIS to pleasure the warriors, where they offer you to the Mujahideen, where you will be shared about the group", say's Imam Tawhidi.

In London Newham, Waltham Forest and Tower Hamlets there are posters on the streets that declare "you are entering a Shari'ah controlled zone: Islamic rules enforced" and Muslim Imams have issued death threats to women who refuse to wear the Hijab. Islamic Emirates Project to turn twelve British cities into "Londonistan" independent states operating under Shari'ah Law and outside of British jurisprudence. Other cities include

Birmingham, Bradford, Derby, Dewsbury, Leeds, Leicester, Liverpool, Luton, Manchester and Sheffield. Sixty-two per cent of Muslim men and seventy-nine per cent of women live on government support and one-third of high security prisons are solely Muslim inmates.

Gordon Brown, once described as the idiot of wall street, declared he wants London to become the Islamic finance capital of the world as most of London's financial institutions are designated Shari'ah compliant. Shari'ah law requires them to donate a portion of the profits to Muslim organizations, for what? and what would this money be used for? David Cameron opined that "multi-culturalism had been a failure" the West had been "cautious, frankly even fearful of standing up to it". He concluded "we have even tolerated these segregated communities behaving in a way that runs completely counter to our values, this hands-off tolerance has only served to reinforce the sense that not enough is shared, what we see and what we see in so many European countries is a process of radicalization".

Anjem Choudary a hate preacher, helped one hundred and ten British Jihadists to travel to Syria, his deputies Mohammed Mizanur Rahman, Mohammed Shamsuddin defended the murder of Lee Rigby by their prodigies Michael Adebolajo and Michael Adebowale, another member of the inner circle Khurram Butt, who led the trio of terrorists involved in the London Bridge tragedy and the Borough Market, all linked to the banned terror group co-founded by Abu Rumaysah, al-Mugjiroun a Salafi Jihadist organisation who can be traced back to the London seven-seven bombings. Anjem Choudary a hate preacher could be freed as early as December 2018 or January 2019! and to return to where back on our streets that's where!

Maajid Nawaz head of the anti-extremist organization the Quillium Foundation say's "Muslim patrols could be a lot more dangerous if it was carried out by Jihadis". Radical Muslim Youths are determined to impose their views of public conduct and morality. In 2014 an American news team accompanied a patrol in action in Ilford, Abu Rumaysah said: "we don't recognise British Law at all, we believe in Islam, we believe in Shari'ah".

Syrian brides for sale, girls are kidnaped and are made to work as prostitutes a recent example of this, girls have been taken from UNHCR camps to be raped and later returned, their ages range from 6 and 7-year-old's and upwards, they are too afraid to go and use the camps toilet blocks at night, this also includes the older women as gangs kidnap them. Men are entering camps dressed as women, the camps have turned to providing vigilante guards in an attempt to protect the women, as UNHCR does not provide camp security.

The men come from the Gulf States, they hide behind the donor authority, they scour the camp during the day and later return to demand a wife, there are no official Islamic marriages, it's a marriage for sexual convenience which lasts days or weeks. The men come from Jordon, Saudi Arabia and Qatar, these camps are seen as marketplaces for selling girls who go for anything between ninety and two-hundred and seventy pounds. A woman interviewed stated that Saudi men would "treat them as a princess" a "pleasure marriage". In Oman, girls go for around eight hundred pounds to get married officially, but after an hour he can divorce her. In Saudi Arabia dowries are very expensive but a Syrian woman is very cheap.

A young Syrian girl from Damascus refused to marry when she was proposed to, her family banned her from going to work, going out, using the telephone and was later tied to a chair and left outside, for fifteen days she was not allowed to move and they whipped her.

The pressures of refugee life created a dramatic rise in domestic violence against women. Jordon provides help for women of domestic violence, offering counselling programmes and centres. Syrian women are "sexually exploited" by aid workers as they trade aid for sex.

Islamic State is driven by the need for total control and absolute power, in order to gain such power, they are using terror to destroy all opposition, this terror is systematic as organized spectacles of punishment of weekly beheadings, burnings and crucifixion at the roadside, this is aimed at a broad an audience as possible to reinforce religious Islamic justice. As they leave a village or town they leave heads on spikes hanging in public spaces. A belief that they will conquer the world, a basic Islamic thought if you do not believe you are not a Muslim and the penalty is death, said the prophet, Mohammed.

IS has lured thousands of foreign fighters and their families with the promise of building a utopian caliphate. The recruiting system is fairly simplistic such as the requirement that men have a skill and that women and girls are not required to have a skill but must be under the age of twenty-six and above all be pretty, where jihadi wives' wannabes sole goal is "I can't wait to have my own jihadi baby".

Several British women now form a police force for ISIS-controlled areas, who make sure that women are covered at all times in public, British women are also involved in running brothels for ISIS fighters and involved in beheadings, referring to them as "boom-boom days" with reference to September eleventh. Some ISIS women say it's the perks of living under the shade of Shari'ah when you can drive past crucified bodies doted along the roadside.

There are hundreds of British jihadi brides wishing to join ISIS but it is reported that for some "it's just too hard" or "I want to come but I'm a full-time mum", but they are being told to "come and bring your kids". Getting married is a synch, as pairing up is very quick, but it's the men who choose when they get to see their face, prospective brides are told to bring something nice to wear because there are no shops, although the women are referred to as female fighters, they are in fact a domestic housewife to be impregnated. Family members have tried to rescue their daughters and sisters who have reported that women are being held against their will, that other women and girls have said "The entire state in which you live would kill you if you said I want to go home" and "Once your there it's for the rest of your life".

The world was created, life began here, Yazidis are an older religion which includes Noah and Adam, who was a Muslim prophet, who is now seen by Muslims as pagan and blasphemous. Yazidis killed or kidnapped by ISIS genocide attacks and indiscriminate deaths and disappearances. The scale of the genocide that was inflicted on the Yazidis by ISIS as they swept through Iraq, members of the ethnic minority were killed or captured, of the nine-thousand some three-thousand were murdered with half executed by gunshot, beheaded or burned alive while the rest died of starvation, dehydration or other injuries. Almost all of the victims who died after fleeing Mount Sinjar were children under the age of fifteen, which also left thousands trapped without food, water and shelter in fifty-degree heat, an act reminiscent of the Armenian atrocities enacted by the Turks.

In Syria the Yazidis are seen as "devil worshipers" due to their links to other religions, ISIS used this in "seeking to erase" the population by group killing, sexual slavery, torture and inhumane treatment by imposing measures to prevent Yazidi children from being born.

Treatment of Afghan women under the Taliban is nothing more than systematic torture and total repression of women. Students of Islam have imposed repressive and draconian measures, psychological and contextual underpinnings with terrifying disturbed views of Islam, that drives such madness that is the plight of women and girls under the Taliban.

The Taliban are driven by a need for total control and absolute power, using terror to paralyse and suppress, at the whim of sadistic gun wielding teenage thugs, every Friday morning at mosque prayers are now followed by weekly beheadings, floggings and amputations and other forms of punishment, which is all done in the name of religion and their right to interpret the teachings of Islam, to dispense their form of justice here on earth for offences against heaven. They impose rule that has made depression and suicidal tendencies a national epidemic among women, who display psychiatric disorders. The Taliban are products of religious schools, funded in part by supporters and individuals in Saudi Arabia, where ultra-strict Wahabi interpretation of the Qur'an, Wahabis repress their women the most.

Taliban list of what is forbidden, music, movies, parties, phones, audio and video, electric razors, any form of entertainment including, toys, kite flying, dolls, card and board games, photographs or pictures of humans or animals, cigarettes, alcohol, magazines, newspapers and most books. The objective being to prevent corrupting people or distracting them from prayer. Women are not allowed to go to school or be treated by male doctors, wear makeup, show any body parts, or wear shoes that make a noise.

The Taliban views women as the "Madonna-whore" fear of women to describe other cultures and religious practices where women are put on pedestals at home but "imprisoned" as potential temptresses. Taliban leader's carryout fanatical extremes as women and girls cannot work outside the home or interact with men who are not relatives, they must be escorted in public by a husband, father, son or brother and must wear the burqa which cover them in dark tents from head to toe, which represents the tents of the desert providing sanctuary as they move about, which must be worn at all times in public. Male taxi drivers cannot take unaccompanied women as a fare no matter how many in number they are.

Other restrictions on women are evermore bizarre, like houses with only women must have all the windows painted black, which imposes further mental and physical health threats due to the lack of natural daylight. Parents are forbidden to teach their daughters to read, the Taliban banned all drawings and images of human beings, thus forcing international health workers to scrap all their educational posters, which was the only way to communicate with largely illiterate women and men.

The Taliban curfew has religious police under the guise of virtue and suppression of vice roam the streets, these gun wielding teenagers who carry antennas or electrical cables, so they can whip any woman they decide is not properly observing their regulations. Women who had once been nurses or teachers, now move in the streets like ghosts under their tent-like robes "burqas", selling any possessions and begging so they can feed their children, legions of women and children are surviving on bread and sugarless tea.

Prior to the Taliban, the Universities were run by mainly women, civil servants and school teachers were also mainly women. Many young women attended University, wore skirts and frequented fashionable street restaurants, discos and walked publicly with their boyfriends. Then the Taliban arrived and excluded women from all public life and public-school education.

Aid workers program to teach women and children how to locate and avoid landmines was stopped by the Taliban, as in their eyes they were using banned pictures of humans and animals and the use of flashcards were outlawed as gambling. The Taliban ended healthcare, women were ordered into segregated hospitals, which had thirty-six beds with no clean or running water, with no electricity, no x-ray facilities or surgical equipment. Female doctors cannot practice healthcare for women and women and girls are dying needlessly. Taliban officials prevent male doctors from undressing women and girls regardless of the fact they will die without treatment, "let them die as those who die on the battlefield".

Taliban guards are posted in hospitals and intervene in the name of the virtue and the vice department have beaten nurses for not being fully covered. On the effects to the health of wearing the burqa, it is especially unhealthy for women afflicted with asthma or hypotension, the burqa can cause eye problems, poor vision, poor hearing, skin rash, headaches, increased cardiac problems, itching scalp, hair loss and depression.

Bathing is outlawed, huge numbers of women do not have access to the "Hamman" the traditional female bath houses, the criticality of these baths in fighting uterine infection after childbirth, which are one in four major causes of maternal mortality and that children under seven years old, who are forced to wash in cold water are in danger of respiratory infections, which is the greatest cause of death in children during the winter months. There is a strong link between health and the ban on women's bathing especially after childbirth, menstruation and intercourse, also every woman is suffering from osteomalacia, the adult form of rickets, due to the lack of vitamin D from wearing the burqa, they survive on a diet of tea and nan bread because they cannot afford eggs and milk.

Ritualistic terror in the form of state-sponsored public punishments is the order of the day. In a weekly ritual hands are amputated by doctors as the mob cheers, these entertainments each week feature, floggings, hangings and beheadings, these are punishments under Taliban law, women are flogged, whipped and beaten to death by being placed in a hole in the ground up to their necks and stones dropped on the head till they die, for wearing white socks. Women marched in protest of the Taliban, as the Taliban surrounded the women they doused their leader in kerosene and burned her alive. Women have been sprayed with acid, shot, beaten for showing their hands while paying for food or allowing their children to play with toys. The Taliban leaders justifies his regime's treatment of women by saying, "A woman's face corrupts men", their total repression is necessary, "otherwise they would be like Princess Diana".

A strange thing happened when going to the forum in Syria in 2016, as you need to be very careful of what you say within public earshot. Anyone who has had children will recognise that for the parents, the need to chastise bad behaviour of their children. A mother was overheard by ISIS jihadists al-Hisbah, the mother said to her daughter "go home" and her four-year-old refused, the mother retorted "go home or by God, I will behead you". The jihadists who heard this beheaded the little girl because the mother invoked the word of God.

A British woman Shukee Begum took her five kids to Turkey and over the border into Syria to get her husband to leave ISIS and return to Britain with them, she was to spend a month in Syria but her money and passport were confiscated so she was trapped.

She spent 10 months under ISIS trying to convince her husband to leave, but he continually refused to do so, her husband a former Guantanamo Bay prisoner, which makes him a serial killer in the eyes of the west, he would not help her to return.

What she had to say about her time in Syria is more poignant "not a place for women and children it's just a dangerous place", she also stated that hundreds of families were living in one home, a safe house, sharing one or two bathrooms and one or two kitchens. The single girls ran the place with a gangster mentality, talking about violence, war and killing and they would huddle around their laptops and watch ISIS videos. She applied to their courts to leave and return to Britain, they said no. She escaped with the help of smugglers then they placed her and her kids in a basement prison for eighty-six days, before being freed and allowed back into Turkey

Chapter 7

Good Bye Jihadist World

Understanding the causes of terrorist behaviour is vital to countering violent extremism, root causes and pathways into terrorist engagement and how terrorist groups fail due to group vulnerabilities, which include internal mistrust through internal power-play, this has a disabling affliction, it focuses energy inward and creates interpersonal tensions and strains relationships. Periods of boredom and inactivity can also threaten group cohesion, that without action and external threat the group may destroy itself. Internal competition and power struggles will undermine group unity, substantive disagreements about tactics, strategy or leadership are sources of vulnerability which leads to fractioning and external pressures create vulnerabilities cumulating in disruption of a support network, disapproval and conflicts with other groups and without a support network, such as the loss of support for, finance, training and weapons all play a part in the downfall of a group.

Preventative strategies or deradicalization have different drivers, as several points of intervention are needed to induce terrorists to break off the process to disengage from a militant group. A more specific and targeted engagement to counter extremist violence is often a gradual process. Life under high pressure and danger over long periods can be the catalyst for change specifically vulnerable to disillusionment, should those within a group not live up to high expectations of loyalty or disappointed by the double standards of their leaders, by demanding sacrifice while leaders enjoy the good life.

Pressure from outside and the fear of infiltration can produce a strong sense of paranoia, this causes individuals to accuse one another of being traitors, the source of scandalous rumours and stories about other members is common in extremist groups, being the prey and hunted by military intelligence or police services is extremely stressful and exhausting.

On another front, others can sway away from the cause, such as Maajid Nawaz the co-founder of the Quilliam Foundation, which works to counter violent extremism and radicalization. He was himself arrested in Egypt and spent years in an Egyptian prison, but no one from the Islamist movement came to his aid, he was just left to fend for himself. It was, therefore, a total surprise to him that Amnesty International came to his aid and fought for his release, this had the effect to turn him away from the path he had chosen.

New significant others can replace bonds in a radicalized group, Saudi Arabia deradicalization program has picked up on the effects that devotion to a romantic partner, or parental obligations for children which promote conflicting loyalties by setting different priorities. Saudi rehabilitation program for Jihadists is culture-specific, a family orientated program by finding prospective spouses in a way of tying them to social commitments. The cost of marriage in Saudi Arabia is very high, the same program for Jihadis also provides help to arrange finance to graduates willing to marry, this is to prevent those who would consider the Jihadist route.

Saudi Arabia has realized the importance of dealing with the religious element of terrorism by other means, that the criminal justice system in their approach which consists of a war of ideas, the aim is to instil moderation and tolerance to undermine the justification for extremism and terrorism. The Saudi government identifies religious schools and religious teaching as a source of extremism which includes Saudi religious schools, to the effect that Imams have been prohibited from incitement and talk of intolerance. The ministry of Islamic Affairs has an educational program to educate Imams and monitor mosques and religious education to purge extremism and intolerance.

In North African Morocco, the government has a comprehensive counter-terrorism strategy that includes vigilant security measures, which is made up of both regional and international cooperation with counter-radicalization policies. The emphasis is on educating and finding employment for the young, its main emphasis is on teaching adherence to the precepts of Islam and Islamic thought by the Maliki School.

The Moroccans hope to counter the appeal of extremist messages and ideologies by reinforcing the influence of the Maliki School by the upgrading the places of worship and at the same time closing unregulated mosques and promoting Moroccan religious values on television and radio and more importantly modernising the teaching of Islam. The development of a curriculum for Imams in countering violent extremism and advancing tolerance, through the use of an Islamic television channel launched by the King of Morocco, which advocates Islamic ideals of tolerance by taking direct aim at jihadist clerics and their media.

In Algeria, the government has multiple law enforcement agencies with delineated responsibilities in counter-terrorism, counter-intelligence and media monitoring. The government does not allow anyone to preach in mosques other than those appointed by the government to do so, which greatly reduces the possibility of importing those who would preach violent Islamist extremist ideologies and prohibits the use of mosques as public meeting places outside of regular prayer hours. Aside from introducing new requirements and training for religious work and a special position for female religious workers "murshidates" the state reasserts its monopoly provision of religious services.

Indonesian citizens discovered that their country was perceived as part of global terrorist network with links to al-Qa'eda, including their terrorist training camp in a remote region of Aceh and their strategy to create a resilient and lethal tactic in imposing a caliphate.

The Indonesian government's recent results of their deradicalization program has shown evidence of positive outcomes regarding terrorists abandoning violence between the concept of disengagement and deradicalization, while deradicalization occurs when an individual no longer believes in a violent ideology. In dealing with this the program it has become essential in the country's counter-terrorism strategy, which includes "hard" and "soft" approaches in the fight against the spread of the jihadi ideology for violent radicalism.

Community youth programmes for young mothers are most effective voices against jihadist warped views and interpretation of Islam. The overwhelming majority of Muslims reject al-Qa'eda, along with Muslim leaders around the world have loudly condemned, al-Qa'eda and its murderous tactics and have declared that it is a violation of Islam to murder innocent people. They also undermine al-Qa'eda's ideology by exposing the lie that it is somehow defending Islamic traditions when in fact, al-Qa'eda violates the basic tenets of Islam. Al-Qa'eda's ideology is undermined by showing that it is the power of nonviolence and democratic change that leads to progress, not senseless terrorism and people of the Arab world are proving the point. Our best defences against this threat are well-informed and equipped families, local communities and institutions. Gang lords and drug dealers, terrorist recruiters prey on those who feel disillusioned or disconnected from their families, community or struggling with their identity and that they must choose between their faith and their country.

Efforts to protect communities against violent extremists must be led by those communities, Islamic scholars have issued, "fatwas", declaring terrorism as un-Islamic and forcefully condemned terrorist attacks and condemning terrorism around the world against people of other faiths, they will not succeed in putting believers of different faiths against one another. For religious minorities the only solution is a programme of education in the ways of peace rather than conflict, there is a growing movement among scholars towards religious dialogue and of their recourse to violence contradicts Islam's ethic of peace and harmony, millions of Muslims condemn terrorist actions committed in the name of Islam. Muslim intellectuals are in the process of rethinking Islam in the face of the challenges of modernity, which has a long tradition of "tajdid" renewal and "islah" reform.

In the fight against jihad, what David Cameron described as "the struggle of our generation", bold measures include giving parents the power to cancel passports of their own children if they suspect they may attempt to join Islamic State, while governments need to target foreign news media that broadcast hate preachers and extremist content. A number of children have been the subject of judicial orders and risk being taken into care because they could be radicalized, interim care orders have been issued to cancel passports.

The manipulation of Islam to target and recruit young people to the terrorist path is "blasphemous" and prohibited, this illustrates how they are destroying Muslim communities, if terrorists are trying to convince young people that they will be joining a winning team, when in fact they have joined a losing one. Muslim youth come from a great tradition that stands for education, not ignorance, not destruction but the dignity of life, not murder. Religious leader's edicts and direct to camera condemnations of terrorism, as terrorist media content often feature prominent terrorists who are not Islamic scholars but make religious claims and use Qur'anic verses out of their proper context to make their recruiting pitch. While Muslims overwhelmingly reject their message, Muslim leaders stress that

ISIL is not Islamic, not a State and not a Caliphate and that joining Daesh is prohibited "haraam" in Islam. The Qur'an emphasizes whoever kills an innocent person it is if he has killed all of humanity.

De-glamorizing Daesh in addition that ISIL is not a Caliphate and highlights Daesh fighters who have retreated and lost ground, debunking foreign fighter lifestyles by showing the miserable living conditions that these fighters have had to endure, such as being forcibly used as janitors and servants, which erodes the terrorist credibility. Muslim voices to graphically illustrate how ISIL, al-Qa'eda and their offshoots are killing mostly Muslims including women and children.

Religious leaders to establish mechanisms for creating content by pan-Arab anti-Daesh within Muslim-majority countries, religious leaders have mobilized as part of a rapid response team of influential figures, such as interventional Imams coming together with a common message supporting effective programmes to establish in every child the principle that violence against the individual is an unacceptable way to address grievances. Broader improvements to educate with enhanced access to education for boys and girls.

Saudi Arabia, Yemen, Singapore, Indonesia and Iraq state that violence against unarmed civilians is unacceptable on religious grounds, this violence will delegitimize it as a means of significant gain, by a handful of kill-happy morons.

Practicing deradicalization that has been implemented in Saudi Arabia, Yemen, Singapore, Iraq, Sri Lanka, and Indonesian efforts have recruited the assistance of Psychologists and other social scientists who have based their practices on sound behavioural principles along with explicit approaches, with the aim to delegitimize the use of violence and introduce an alternative means by the significant use of alternative goals.

Muslim clerics who engage in a theological dialogue as to the correct interpretation of the Qur'an, which does not condone violence against non-believers which views jihad as primarily an integral struggle for goodness and virtue, rather than a violent fight against infidels.

Involving the families of detainees in the rehabilitation process represents another implicit way of activating nonideological concerns incompatible with violent sacrifice for a cause. Despite the perceptual variability in radicalization, the social process network and group dynamics and the need for cognitive closure can provide a solution.

Australian Muslim women with the opportunities to enable them to actively participate in and contribute to Australia's cultural and religiously diverse society, Muslim women expanded the scope of their activities to include interfaith dialogue. The Muslim women's Support Centre has been organising awareness among their number in "the Australian lifestyle" to help them make a positive contribution to Australian society without losing their identity. It is also assisting the Muslim community in finding ways to address issues such as domestic violence, parenting and finding foster parents for Muslim children.

Muslim women's groups which combine their Islamic Australian and ethnic identities as the basis for promoting citizenship with the emphasis in living within an Australian liberal democracy and concerned about the possibility of "homegrown" militancy being replicated in Australia; the federal government has embarked upon a progression of engaging the Muslim community.

As the war on terror progressed in Syria in 2017, the utopian ideal became a rapidly evaporating caliphate, as their ravaged health care system bombed by Russia and Iran into rubble. The lifestyles of the terrorist fighters and their supporters began to take its toll, with the outbreak of sexually transmitted diseases such HIV within their ranks, while testing equipment had been sourced and put in place male doctors refused medical care to women seeking treatment without a male guardian.

Blood transfers between fighters without prior analysis for contagious diseases are the driver to an increased risk of HIV.

The prevalence of injecting jihadi drugs between local fighters and having short-term marriages results in a high turnover of partners. The problem with one day marriages or new marriage patterns are a real concern given the spread of HIV, a lot of foreign fighters are getting married for just a few months, in some cases lasting a day, then divorcing or dying in battle leaves a wider population fighting HIV, with no healthcare system and destroyed hospitals the spread of disease will be out of control for years.

Epilogue

The prophet Mohammed was an innovator who gave women legal status such as property and inheritance rights, his closest confidants were women, his first convert was his wife Khadija an independent businesswoman. The punishments in Saudi Arabia of beheadings and floggings are tribal relics of a pre-Islamist past when nomadic tribesmen-maintained order by lopping off the hands of thieves and beheading of murderers, the use of blood money intended to prevent blood feuds as there are "no jails in a desert".

Islam also dictates equal and mandatory education, under Mohammed women scholars became teachers to prominent men, the medical army were all female and women participated in public affairs involved in the negotiating of treaties and some were even judges. As for dress code, only Mohammed's wives were required to cover their faces, and women undertaking the "hajj" pilgrimage to Mecca are to do so with their faces uncovered. Mohammed taught "there is no compulsion in Islam". Muslim scholars say the Taliban's laws and rules and teachings that have been put into practice in several countries has nothing to do with Islam.

Protecting civil rights by vigorously enforcing new hate crime laws in the wake of terrorist attacks, instead of condemning whole communities we need to join with those communities to help themselves as well, should one faith community face intimidation we need to come together. Many incidents do not make headlines because of good citizenship and patriotism of Muslims, who noticed something and spoke out, cooperation from Muslims has been absolutely essential in identifying and preventing terrorist threats. Local communities need to build their own capacity to disrupt, challenge and counter terrorist propaganda in both the real and virtual world.

The role of women in supporting the government to confront terrorism is enormous and the empowerment of women in preventing the terrorist action is the best form of "soft" power. Women have the power to fight terrorism, therefore, women can become bastions to maintain peace in the world, to counter terrorism women must be educated to act and the use of the burka must be seen as a barrier to that end.

It should be made an offence under British law, that any female citizen should not be subjugare[16] to wearing either the Niqab a veil that covers the face showing only the eyes, or the Taliban-Wahhabi inspired Burka a full-face and full-body covering nor the Iranian Chador full-body cloak likewise wearing

---

[16] Under the Yoke

a Balaklava is unacceptable, a male walking down a street wearing this head covering is not out for a stroll and should be reported to the police. Muslim men or Imams who force women to these non-British forms of appeasement should be treated as though they are committing acts equal to controlling and coercive subjugation, domestic violence and domestic abuse.

Controlling or coercing behaviour in an intimate or family relationship! Comes under the Serious Crime Act 2015 sec 76.

"This offence is constituted by behaviour on the part of the perpetrator which takes place "repeatedly or continuously". The victim and alleged perpetrator must be "personally connected" at the time the behaviour takes place. The behaviour must have had a "serious effect" on the victim, meaning that it has caused the victim to fear violence will be used against them on "at least two occasions" or it has had a "substantial adverse effect on the victims' day to day activities". The alleged perpetrator must have known that their behaviour would have a serious effect on the victim, or the behaviour must have been such that he or she "ought to have known" it would have that effect. Controlling or coercive behaviour should be dealt with as part of adult and or child safeguarding and public protection procedures".

Muslim's and other immigrants must be asked to take Citizenship, otherwise, it should be mandatory that they must relocate to another country, financial help for this should be given. All terrorist or potential terrorist, hate preaching Muslim prisoners should not be allowed back into society on their release, but be deported elsewhere, unless they have a birth right and can therefore be placed on a register of offenders.

Shari´ah-compliant financial institutions are required to donate a portion of the profits to Muslim organizations designated by their Shari´ah advisors. Should this be allowed to continue, it cannot be simply being allowed to vanish into the aether[17] but be totally transparent, who for and for what purpose, in Britain best donated to the NHS.

British Islamic institutions and the Roman Catholic Church, the Church of Scotland, the Church of England, Hindu, Mormon and other faith groups should be controlled by the relevant religious councils in Britain. All religious faiths should have a register of all those who are fit and proper and are licenced to practice as worship leaders, teachers or who head local religious groups. They must be trained and their performance monitored for extremes such as sexual deviancy, coercion and hate preaching. Islamic buildings Mosques and community centres application to local authorities to build should be through the Muslim Council of Britain, no Muslim Caliphates within Britain, no Arabic estates or towns, streets, avenues or road names joint or otherwise to be given planning permission or

---

[17] Into the air

allowed under any circumstance. No Shari'ah law-controlled zones.

Muslim communities must come under the laws of the land in the countries that they live in, Muslin women must be taught that country's language that they have settled in, with no segregated communities. Imams to be educated and monitored, religious education and mosques must be monitored and if necessary prayers should no longer be given in Arabic. Prohibit mosques as meeting places outside of regular prayer hours and no unregulated mosques. Promote Islamic religious values on television and radio, for advancing tolerance with a programme of education in the ways of peace and harmony in countering violent extremism.

On the twenty-eighth of January 2018, the EU council refused to discuss the subject of Jihadi brides returning to EU territories. Two Londoners former ISIS fighters captured in Syria, El Shafee el-Sheikh and Alexander Kotey who had been stripped of their British citizenship, are desperately trying to return to Britain but the UK defence secretary does not want them returned, it was reported that "they are not British subjects and should pay the price for their crimes in Syria", eight hundred and fifty Britons joined ISIS in Syria and Iraq and some four hundred have since returned. In Britain if we have to take back these terrorists to conform with international law, then we should build a prison on South Georgia for their enjoyment.

Source Material
Bibliography

Prologue

Holt, P.M., Lewis, B, (1977) Cambridge History of Islam, Vol. 1. Cambridge University press.

Sonn, T., (2004) "A Brief History of Islam" Blackwell Publishing.

Roger, S., (2012) "The Encyclopaedia of Ancient History" Wiley-Blackwell.

Chapter 1

Al-Mazroui group aims supply of investments in health, housing, and Suez Canal. (2014, Nov 25). *Daily News Egypt.*

Alonso, R. Ray, MG., (2007) The evolution of Jihadist terrorism in Morocco: Terrorism & Political Violence pp 571-592.

Algeria (2010) Lanham: Federal Information & News Despatch Inc.

Arieff, A., (2012) Morocco Current Issues. Current Politics and Economics of Africa 5 (2) pp 225-287.

Background Notes: Djibouti. (2010) Lanham: Federal Information & News Despatch, Inc.

Belay, G.F., (2013) A review of Ethiopia's Security Challenges in the Horn of Africa. Army War Coll Carlisle Barracks PA.

Coptic solidarity; congressional delegation declares solidarity with Egypt against terrorism. (2013). *Bioterrorism Week.*
Country specific information Egypt. (2008). (). Lanham: Federal Information & News Dispatch, Inc.

Devi, S., (2017). Troubling times for health and human rights in Egypt. *The Lancet, 389*(10070), pp 686-687.

Garamone, J., (2012). *Al-Qaida offshoots are biggest terror threat, official says.* (). Lanham: Federal Information & News Dispatch, Inc.

Gidey, T.A., (2012) Ethiopian-Eritrea conflict: Security Implications for the Horn of Africa. Army War Coll Carlisle Barracks PA.

Gulf of Aden Counter-Terrorism Forum, February 3-5, 2014, Djibouti (2014). Lanham; Federal Information & News Dispatch, Inc.

Howe, M., (2005) Morocco: the Islamist awakening and other challenges: Oxford University Press.

Human rights conditions in Egypt. (2015). (). Lanham: Federal Information & News Dispatch, Inc.

Kartas, M., (2011) On the Edge? Trafficking and Insecurity at the Tunisian–Libyan Border.

Kimunguyi, P., (2011) Terrorism and Counter Terrorism in East Africa. Global Terrorism Research Centre Monash University Australia.

Leonardi, C., (2011) Paying "buckets of blood" for the land: Moral debates over economy, war and the state in Southern Sudan. The Journal of Modern African Studies, 49 (2) pp 215-240.

Litewicka, P., (2016) Using life history approach to explore the current Eritrean refuge crisis.

Lewis, I.M., Lewis, I., ASCAP and Dwyer, MJ (2008) Understanding Somalia and Somaliland: Culture, History, Society. New York: Columbia University Press.

Mekonnen, D.R., and Tesfagioris, P. (2011) The cause and consequences of the Eritrean-Ethiopian border conflict. Regional Security in the post-Cold War Horn of Africa, p 65.

Migdalovitz, C., (2010 Feb) Morocco: Current Issues. Library of Congress Washington DC Congressional Research Service.

Moghaddam, F.M., (2006) From the terrorist point of view: What they experience and why they come to destroy. Greenwood Publishing Group.

Nzaw, M (2010) Counter-Terrorism in the Greater Horn of Africa 2004-10; Revisiting the Somalia Question. Journal of

Language, Technology & Entrepreneurship in Africa 2 (2), pp 163-167

Patey, L.A., (2010) Crude Days Ahead? Oil and the resource curse in Sudan. African Affairs 109 (437) pp 617-636.

Remarks at the U.S.-Egypt strategic dialogue. (2015). (). Lanham: Federal Information & News Dispatch, Inc.

Rodriguez, R.M., (2015) The Conflict Between Ethiopia and Eritrean Assessment and Political Solutions. Lulu Press Inc.

Siddig, K.H., (2011) Oil and Agriculture in the post separation of the Sudan.

Terrorist designation of Said Arif Lanham: Federal Information & News Despatch Inc.

Terrorism; studies from university of Bristol in the area of terrorism published. (2012). *Bioterrorism Week,* 19.

The Re-Designation of Al-Qaeda in the Islamic Maghreb as a foreign terrorist organization. Federal Information & News Despatch Inc.

The role of women in overcoming Egypt's economic and security challenges in the 21st century. (2016). (). Lanham: Federal Information & News Dispatch, Inc.

U.S. Bilateral Relations Fact Sheets: Djibouti 2013. Lanham: Information & News Dispatch, Inc.

US: Declares Moroccan group a foreign terrorist organization (2005) Lanham: Federal Information and News Despatch Inc.

Walret, A., (2017) Governance, violence and the struggle for economic regulation in South Sudan: the case of Budi country (Eastern Equatoria) Africa Focus, 21 (2).

Chapter 2

Ahmed, F., (1993) The Making of Modern Turkey: Taylor & Francis e-Library 2003.

Al-Rasheed., (2010) A History of Saudi Arabia. Cambridge University Press, 2nd ed.

Anonymous (2013) Nov 25th. Chemical Warfare: Researchers from Tehran University of Medical Sciences Report New Studies and Findings in the Area of Chemical Warfare. Bioterrorism week 18. ISSN 15478602.

Avedian, V., (2012) State Identity, Continuity and Responsibility: The Ottoman Empire, the Republic of Turkey and the Armenian Genocide: European Journal of International Law, Volume 23 (3), pp 797-820.

Background notes: Iraq (2011) Lanham: Federal Information and News Dispatch, Inc

Bose, S., Jalal, A., (2017) Modern South Asia: history, culture, political economy. Routledge.

Burak, B., (2011) The Role of the Military in Turkish Politics; "To Guard Whom and from What?": European Journal of Economic and Political Studies, Volume 4 (1) pp 143-170.

Carpenter, T.G., (2013) Tangled Web: The Syrian War and its Implications: Mediterranean Quarterly, 24 (1).

Dinar, A., (2011) The Justice and Development Party: Turkey's experience with Islam, Democracy, Liberalism, and Secularism: Journal of Middle East Studies, 43 pp 529-541.

Dorroll, P., (2014) "The Turkish Understanding of Religion": Rethinking Tradition and Modernity in Contemporary Turkish Islamic Thought; Journal of the American Academy of Religion, Volume 82, 4, pp 1033-1069.

Dressler, J.A., (2010) The Haqqani Network: from Pakistan to Afghanistan. Institute for the Study of War.

Fair, C.C., (2015) Explaining support for sectarian terrorism in Pakistan: Piety, Maslak and Sharia. Religions, 6(4) pp 1137-67.

Gökaniksel, B., Secor, A., (2014) Post-secular geographies and the problem of pluralism; Religion and everyday life in Istanbul Turkey; Journal of Political Geography, 43 pp21-30.

Goodson, L.P., (2014) The new great game: Pakistan's Approach to Afghanistan after 2014. Asia Policy No 17 pp 33-39 National Bureau of Asian Research.

Göl, A., (2017) The Paradoxes of "new" Turkey: Islam, illiberal democracy and republicanism. International Affairs, Volume 93(4) pp 957-966.

Griffiths, A.L., (2002) Observations on Americans and War. Peace and Conflict: Journal of Peace Psychology, 8(4), pp 95-97

Gunter, M.M., (2015) Iraq, Syria, ISIS and the Kurds: Geostrategic concerns for the US and Turkey: Middle East Policy, 22(1), pp 102-111.

Hameed, S., (2017) The Arab Awakening: America and the Transformation of the Middle East: Africa Review Volume 9(1).

Hegghammer, T., (2008) Islamist Violence and Regime Stability in Saudi Arabia. International Affairs, Vol 84, Nº 4 pp 701-755

Hertog, S., (2001) Princes, Brokers and Bureaucrats: Oil and the State in Saudi Arabia: Cornell University Press.

Humud, C.E., Blanchard, C.M., Nikitin, M.B.D., (2017) Armed Conflict in Syria: Overview and US response: Congressional Research Service Washington United States.

Jäckle, S., Baumann, M., (2017) New terrorism = higher brutality? An empirical test of the brutalization thesis. Terrorism and Political Violence, 29(5) pp 875-901.

Keyman, E.F., (2007) Modernity, Secularism and Islam; The Case of Turkey: Journal Theory, Culture & Society Vol 24(20), pp 215-234.

Lawson, F.H., (2014) Syria's mutating civil war and its impact on Turkey, Iraq and Iran: International Affairs, 90(6), pp 1351-1356.

Mousari, M.D., Soroush, M.R., et al (2015) Epidemiological Study of Child Casualties of Landmines and unexploded Ordnances: A National Study from Iran. Prehospital and Disaster Medicine, 30(5), pp 472-477.

Niblock, T., Malik, M., (2007) The Political Economy of Saudi Arabia, London UK, Routledge.

Peters, G., (2012) Haqqani Network Financing: The Evolution of an Industry. Combating Terrorism Centre, United States Military Academy West Point.

Rassler, D., Brown, V., (2011) The Haqqani Nexus and the evolution of al-Qa'eda. Combatting Terrorism Centre, United States Military Academy West Point.

Sathasivan, K., (2017) Uneasy Neighbours: India, Pakistan and US foreign policy. Routledge.

Shah, S.W.A., (2017) Political Reforms in the Federally Administered Tribal Area of Pakistan (FETA): Will it end the current militancy? Heidelberg Papers in South Asia and Comparative Politics (64).

Sharp, D., (2006) Long-term effects of Sarin. The Lancet, 367(9505), pp 95-97.

Siddiqa, A., (2017) Military Inc: inside Pakistan's military economy. Penguin Random House India.

Sovleimanor E.A., (2014) Globalizing Jihad? North Caucasians in Syrian Civil War. Middle East Policy, 21(3), pp 154-162.

Yildiz, A.A., Verkuyten, M., (2011) Inclusive Victimhood: Social identity and the politicization of collective trauma among Turkey's Alevi's in Western Europe. Peace & Conflict: Journal of Peace Psychology, 17(3), pp 243-269.

Chapter 3

Al-Momani et al (2010) Political Participation of Muslims in Australia, Centre for Research on Social Inclusion, Macquarie University Australia.

Al Qurtuby, S., (2017) "Arabs and "Indo-Arabs" in Indonesia: Historical Dynamics, Social Relations and Contempory Changes" International Journal of Asia-Pacific Studies 13(2) pp 45-72.

Crouch, M., (2009) Indonesia, Militant Islam and Ahmadiyah: Origins and Implications. Centre for Islamic Law and Society, University of Melbourne. ARC Islam, Shari'ah and Governance Background Paper.

Davies, M.N., (2006) Indonesia's War over Aceh: Last stand on Macca's porch. Politics in Asia, Routledge Taylor & Francis.

Kka Putra, I., Sukabdi, Z.A., Basic concepts and reasons behind the emergence of religious terror activities in Indonesia: An inside view. Asian Journal of Social Psychology 16 pp 83-91.

Lion, J.C., (2014) ISIS Goes to Asia: Extremists in the Middle East Isn't Only Spreading West. Council of Foreign Affairs.

Gross, M.L., (2017) A Muslim archipelago: Islam and Politics in Southeast Asia. Government Printing Office.

Hadiz, V.R., Teik, K.B., (2011) Approaching Islam and politics from political economy: A comparative study of Indonesia and Malaysia. The Pacific Review, 24(4) pp 463–485.

Jayakumar, S., (2017) The Islamic State Looks East: The Growing Threat in Southeast Asia, CTS Sentinel 22.

Kabir, N., (2007) Muslims in Australia: The double edged of terrorism. Journal of Ethnic and Migration Studies, 33(8) pp 1277–1297.

McCormack, L., McKellar, L., (2015) Adaptive growth following terrorism: Vigilance and anger as facilitators of posttraumatic growth in the aftermath of the Bali bombings. Traumatology: An International Journal, 21(2), pp 78-81.

Mullins, S., (2011) Islamist Terrorism and Australia: An Empirical Examination of the "Home Grown" Threat. Terrorism and Political Violence, 23(2), pp 254–285.

Rabasa, A., (2014) Political Islam in Southeast Asia: Moderates, Radical and Terrorists (No38) Routledge.

Ramakrishna, K., (2017) The Growth of ISIS Extremism in Southeast Asia: Its ideological and Cognitive Features and Possible Policy Responses. New England Journal of Public Policy 29(1) p 6.

Robinson, G., (2010) State – Sponsored Violence and Secessionist Rebellions in Asia. The Oxford Handbook of Genocide Studies.

Stumpter, C., (2017) Countering violent extremism in Indonesia: priorities, practice and the role of civil society. Journal for Deradicalization, Summer 2017 Nr 11.

Webster, D., (2018) Flowers in the wall: Truth and Reconciliation in Timor – Leste, Indonesia and Melanesia.

Weintraub, J., (2017) Factors influencing the movement of Southeast Asian Fighters to ISIS: A comparison of Indonesia and Malaysia (Doctoral dissertation, Cornell University).

Weiss, M.L., (2010) "Malaysia – Indonesia bilateral Relations: Sibling rivals in a fraught Family" International relations in Southeast Asia: Between bilateralism and Multilaterism, pp 171–198.

Yang Hui, J., (2010) The Internet in Indonesia: Development and impact of Radical Websites. Studies in Conflict & Terrorism, 33: pp 171-191 Routledge Taylor Francis.

Chapter 4

Al Hassan, Y.N., et al (2016) Belief systems enforcing female genital mutilation in Europe. International Journal of Human Rights in Healthcare 9(1) pp 29-40.

Aplin, R.L., (2018) Honour based abuse: the response by professionals to vulnerable adult investigations. Journal of Aggression, Conflict and Peace Research.

Bartels, S.A., et al (2018) Making sense of child, early and forced marriage among Syrian refugee girls: A mixed methods study in Lebanon. BMJ Global Health 3(1) p.e. 000509.

Brinkmann, K., (2018) Why sixteen million bonded labourers remain invisible: What Althusser has to say. Advances in Applied Sociology 8(01) p 49.

Chantler, K., (2012) Recognition of and intervention in forced marriage as a form of violence and abuse. Trauma, Violence & Abuse 12(3) pp 176–183.

Davy, D., (2018) Trafficking of vulnerable children in Southeast Asia. In Assisting Young Children Caught in Disasters pp 47–55. Springer Cham.

Erulkar, A., (2013) Early marriage, marital relations and intimate partner violence in Ethiopia. International Perspectives on Sexual and Reproductive Health. Pp 6–13.

Haworth, A., (2012) Observer Magazine: The Day I Saw 248 Girls Being Circumcised: In 2006, while in Indonesia and six months pregnant, Abigail Haworth became one of the few journalists ever to see young girls suffering genital mutilation, until now she has been unable to tell this shocking story. The Observer 30 ISSN 00297712.

Khan, R., Saleem, S., Lowe, M., (2018) "Honour" – based violence in a British South Asian community. Safer Communities 17(1) pp 11–21.

Khan, R., (2018) Attitudes towards "Honour" violence and killings in collectivist cultures: The Routledge International Handbook of Human Aggression: Current Issues and Perspectives.

Martino, M.G., Papastathis, K., (2018) The Radical Right and Religious Discourse. In Das Narrative von der Wielder der Religion. pp 261–287 Springer VS Wiesbaden.

Rosoult, H.R., Ebrahini, A., Motamedi, M.H.K., (2015) Raising awareness against acid attacks. The Lancet 385 (9970) pp 772-773.

Sable, A., et al (2013) Determinants of child and forced marriage in Morocco: stakeholder perspectives on health, policies and human rights. B.M.C. International health and human rights.

Chapter 5

Ahmad, F., et al (2012) Information propagation and the forces of social media in Malaysia, Asian Social Science 8(5) p 71.

Atran, S., (2006) "The Moral Logic and Growth of Suicide Terrorism". The Washington Quarterly, Centre for Strategic and Intelligence Studies, MIT,2006,29, PP.127-147.

Bermingham, A., (2008) "Combining Social Network Analysis and Sentiment Analysis to Explore the Potential for Online Radicalization. Science foundation Ireland 07/CE/11147, Enterprise Ireland IP/2008/0549.

Borum, R., (2010) "Understanding Terrorist Psychology" Mental Health Law & Policy. Faculty Publications usf.edu Paper 576.

Bouhana, N., Wikström, P.O.H., (2011) Al-Qa'eda-influenced radicalization: A rapid evidence assessment guided by Situational Action Theory. Scientific report, UK Home Office.

Cherney, A., Murphy, K., (2016) Being a "suspect community" in a post 9/11 world: The Impact of the war on terror on Muslim communities in Australia. Australia & New Zealand Journal of Criminology, 49(4) pp 480–496.

Gilluffo, F.S., et al (2010) Foreign Fighters: Trajectories & Conflict Zones, Homeland Security Policy Institute, George Washington University.

Greitemeyer, T, McLatche, N, (2011) "Denying Humanness to Others": A Newly Discovered Mechanism by which Violent Video Games Increase Aggressive Behaviour. Department of Psychology, university of Innsbruck, sagepub.com.

Hassan, R., (2010) "Socio-economic marginalisation of Muslims in contemporary Australia: "Implications for Social inclusion" Journal of Muslim minority affairs. 30(4) pp 575–584.

Hassan, R., (2015) Australian Muslims: A demographic, social and economic profile of Muslims in Australia: University of South Australia.

Hopkins, L., McAuliffe, C., (2010) Split allegiances: Cultural Muslims and the tensions between religious and national identity in multicultural societies. Studies in Ethnicity and Nationalism 10(1) pp 38–58.

Kruglanski, A., et al (2014) "The Psychology of Radicalisation and Deradicalization: How significance Quest Impacts Violent Extremism". Advances in Political Psychology, vol35, supplement, 1, 2014.

McGill University, (2011) Terrorism: Findings in terrorism reported from McGill University. Bioterrorism week, 11. ISN 15478602.

Milgram, S., (1963) Behavioural Study of Obedience. Journal of Abnormal and Social Psychology, 67, 371-378.

Milgram, S., (1965) Some Conditions of Obedience and Disobedience to Authority, Human Relations, 18, 57-76.

Milgram, S., (1974) Obedience to Authority, New York, Harper & Row.

Putra, I.E., Sukabdi, Z.A., (2014) Can Islamic fundamentalist relate to nonviolent support? The role of certain conditions in moderating the effect of Islamic fundamentalism on supporting acts of terrorism. Peace and Conflict: Journal of peace Psychology, 20(4), pp 583-589.

Shapiro, J.N., Fair. C.C., (2010) Understanding support for Islamist Militancy in Pakistan. International Security Vol 34 (3) pp 79-118 Harvard and Massachusetts Institute of Technology.

Thompson, R.L., (2012) "Radicalization and the use of Social Media" Journal of Strategic Security Volume 4, No4, Winter 2011, 167-190.

Chapter 6

Asra Batool, S., Ahmed, H.K., Qureshi, S.N., (2018) Impact of demographic variables on women's economic empowerment: An ordered probity model. Journal of Women & Aging, 30 (1) pp 6–26.

Callimachi, R., (2016) IS uses contraceptives to maintain sexual slavery. The Hindu ISSN 097175X.

Hegghammer, T., (2008) Islamist Violence and Regime Stability in Saudi Arabia. International Affairs Vol 84 (4) pp 701-705.

Litewnicka, P., (2016) Using life history approach to explore the current Eritrean refugee crisis. University of Porto.

McAlpine, A., Hossain, M., Zimmerman, C., (2016) Sex trafficking and sexual exploitation in settings affected by armed conflicts in Africa, Asia and the Middle East: Systematic review BMC International Health and Human Rights 16.

Rukmini, C.D., (2016) Forced birth control revealed. The Age 13 ISSN 03126307.

Stenersen, A., (2010) The Taliban insurgency in Afghanistan organization, leadership and worldwide. Norwegian Defence Research Establishment (FFI).

Suarez, P.A., (2018) Child – Bride marriage and female welfare. European Journal of Law and Economics pp 1–28

Yasin, B.A., et al (2013) Female genital mutilation among Iraqi Kurdish women: a cross sectional study from Irbil City. BMC Public Health 13 pp 809.

Yigit, S., (2017) The women of Afghanistan: Past and present challenges. Journal of social studies, Vol (2).

Chapter 7

Ahmad, L., Anctil Avoine, P., (2018) Misogyny in "post-war Afghanistan: the changing frames of sexual and gender-based violence. Journal of Gender Studies 27(1) pp 86-101.

Ahmad, M.Z., Kelana, M., (2017) An Inter-State Maritime Territorial Conflict: A Study on Malaysia's Conflict Resolution Trough Peaceful Means. Sosiohumanionra 7(2) p 92.

Chatterjee, P., (2011) Campaigns against acid violence spur change, World Health Organisation. Bulletin of the World Health Organization 89(1) pp 6-7.

Clark, J.D., et al (2017) The shifting landscape of global internet censorship.

Ebeturk, I.A., Cowart, O., (2017) Criminalization in forced marriage in Europe: A qualitative comparative analysis. International Journal of Comparative Sociology 58(3) pp 169–191.

Febrica, S., (2015) Why Cooperate? Indonesia and Anti-Maritime Terrorism Cooperation. Asian Politics & Policy 7(1) pp 105-130.

Febrica, S., (2017) Maritime Security and Indonesia: Cooperation Interests and Strategies (vol. 86) Taylor & Francis.

Fenton, A.J., Price, D., (2015) Breaking ISIS: Indonesia's legal position on the "Foreign Terrorist Fighters" threat.

Global Counterterrorism Forum Co-Chairs: About the Global Counterterrorism Forum (GCTF) (2014) Washington: Federal Information News Dispatch, Inc.

Hong, N., Ng, A.K., (2010) The international legal instruments in addressing piracy and maritime terrorism: A critical review, Research in Transportation Economics, 27(1) pp 51-60.

Knight, F., (2014) Forced Marriage: Engaging with Renegotiations Within. In Law, Power and Culture. pp 146–166 Palgrave London.

Morse, J., (2006) Iran the "Central Banker for Terrorism" in the Middle East, Rice say's: Secretary lauds Indonesia for its "voice of moderation" in the Islamic World. Washington: Federal Information News Dispatch, Inc.

Muhammad, A., (2017) International Context Indonesia's Counter Terrorism Policy 2001-2004, Journal IL Miah Hubungan International 8(2).

Muvill, N., et al (2018) "The experience of interactional justice for victims of "honour" – based violence and abuse reporting to the Police in England and Wales". Policing and Society pp 1–17.

Nethery, A., Gordyn, C., (2014) Australia – Indonesia cooperation on asylum seekers: a case of "incentivised policy transfer" Australian Journal of Internal Affairs, 68(2) pp 177–193.

Rabasa, A., et al (2010) Deradicalizing Islamist Extremists. RAND National Security Research Division.

Singh, A., (2011) India-Malaysia Strategic Relations Maritime Affairs: Journal of the National Maritime Foundation of India 7(1) pp 85-105.

Sundaram, L., Travers, E., Branson, M., (2018) How to end child marriage around the world. Handbook of Adolescent Development Research and its Impact on Global Policy. P 173.

Stern, J., (2010) Mind over Martyr: How to deradicalize Islamist extremists. Foreign Affairs. pp 9 –108.